Hidden Credit Repair Secrets

That Fix Your Credit In 30 Days

First Edition

Mark Clayborne

Board Certified Credit Consultant

www.hiddencreditrepairsecrets.com

Get Results Through Proven Credit Restoration Techniques

Hidden Credit Repair Secrets

Printed by Create Space

ISBN 9781456321345

Cover illustration: Imagetrance www.imagetrance.com

First edition published 2010

Manufactured in the United States of America.

This product is not a substitute for legal advice.

Visit us at hiddencreditrepairsecrets.com

Table of Contents

Chapter 3: When the Credit Bureaus Won't Fix My Credit Report 53

Chapter 4: Removing the "Eleven Killers" From My Credit Report...........60

Chapter 5: How to Repair My Credit With Debt Settlement Techniques......88

Chapter 6: Can I Stop the Collection Agterns in Their Tracks? 100

Chapter 7: How Can I Protect My Good Credit During a Divorce? 112

Chapter 8: Rebuilding My Credit From the Ground Up 121

Chapter 9: Raising My Credit Score..134

Chapter 10: Should I File for Bankruptcy? 148

Chapter 11: Suing the Credit Bureaus to get them to remove negative information from my credit report 157

DISCLAIMER

PREFACE

Learning how to repair my credit and credit score has been a rewarding experience. It has provided me with opportunities to receive credit without any roadblocks, but it has not always been that way. In 1995, I was 23 and had just graduated from college with a B.A. in Criminal Justice and impeccable credit. I moved to New York City to pursue my career in Law Enforcement and Filmmaking. While searching for a job, I started studying various ways of making a film. During my filmmaking research, I realized that making independent films required large amounts of funding, and as a struggling student, I was uncertain where I would find the money. Well, I knew that my credit score at the time was 700, so I could just borrow a personal loan. After thinking about it for a few weeks, I went to a bank and applied for a $15,000 unsecured loan (no collateral required) and was quickly approved. From there, I proceeded to start making my film, but quickly ran out of money. I went back to the same bank and applied for a $5000 credit card and was approved again. This cycle repeated itself as I continued to run out of money and apply for more credit at different banks until eventually I was in over my head with debt.

Upon completion of the film, a year later, I wondered to myself how I would ever pay off all of my debt, especially since my debt exceeded my annual income. For the first year and a half, I was making my payments on time trying to maintain my good credit score. Then, all of sudden, I started becoming 30 days late, 60 days late, even 120 days behind. I had so many payments. I could hardly pay some of my basic bills. I was frustrated and stressed with nowhere to turn, so I tried the consumer credit counseling for relief. They helped cut down the interest on the credit cards and assisted me with making my monthly payments. Then, there was a job change and a relocation of my address. Since I was out of work for a short period of time, it caused me to default on my credit consumer obligations. At this point, I was tired and upset with the debt, so just I gave up. When this happened, things got worse, all of my credit cards went into a charge off status and to collection agencies, my tax preparer messed up my taxes causing me to owe back taxes, which eventually turned into a tax lien. Bill collectors were calling every day. Three credit judgments were entered by default because I was not present at court due to not receiving the court notice. And finally, the financial difficulties were causing problems with my relationship. In conclusion, I had no choice but to file bankruptcy, which dropped my score by almost 100 points.

During my first year of bankruptcy, I could not get approved for a new apartment, a cell phone, basic utilities, store credit cards, or anything pertaining to credit. I was not happy. I couldn't even apply to work for the police department until after three years of the bankruptcy had been discharged. I knew I couldn't live like this for the next 10 years, which is the amount of time the bankruptcy takes to come off of your report. So I began my journey on how to rebuild my credit report and take my financial life back. I immediately called a friend of mine for the contact information of a credit repair company he had used to assist him with his credit. I signed up with the firm and the company started the repair process, but something soon happened that kind of shocked me. I received the credit repair firm dispute letter by mistake. Instead of mailing the dispute letter to the credit bureau, they mailed it to me. I carefully read the letter trying to understand the credit repair firm's language that forced the credit bureaus to remove negative items from my credit report. Months went by, and another letter came to me. Then another one. I called the firm and advised them that their letters were coming to me and instead of to the credit bureaus. They apologized and stated that it wouldn't happen again, but by this time I had already accumulated about ten of their letters. Throughout the next six months, I called the firm up almost every day asking them various questions on credit repair and credit scores. After questioning them to death, I felt that I was knowledgeable enough to take a shot at repairing my own credit.

By the time I canceled with the credit repair company, they had removed six or seven items off of my credit report, but I still had many more included in the bankruptcy. I continued the dispute process on my own and started seeing improvements within the first month alone. It was encouraging, and by seeing how easily the letters worked, I even began to like the whole concept of credit repair. From then on, I went to classes on credit repair, credit scoring, bankruptcy, divorce and credit, foreclosures, small claims court, and debt settlement. I read every book and article I could find on the credit scoring and credit repair process. Eventually, I went through extensive training with Credit Consultant Association to obtain my Board Certification as a Credit Consultant. With my extensive knowledge on credit repair, I was able to remove every derogatory item on my credit report and take my score from a disheartening 540 to an impressive 700. Once my family and friends got a wind of my skills on credit repair, they all wanted help. But I was not satisfied with helping only my close friends and family members improve their financial situation. I knew that millions of people suffer from poor credit every year without knowing where to turn. This is why I took my years of experience on credit repair and created Hidden Credit Repair Secrets, to help you change your financial situation forever.

CHAPTER 1:

Understanding Credit Reports

Patty's story

While I was getting ready to start my work shift, Patty, a co-worker stated to me, "I understand you're writing a book on credit repair." She went on to say that she had applied for cable and a cell phone and was required to put down anywhere from $100 to $300 deposit. I asked her why she was required to put down a deposit, but she wasn't sure. Then I asked her for the last time she checked her credit report, but she also did not know. Patty went on to say that she owed the bank money, and now whenever she tries to open a checking account she gets denied. "I don't know what to do Mark!" I told her, "It's not the end of the world, Patty. You just need a little guidance. First, you definitely need to get a copy of your credit report." I told her how to get a copy from annualcreditreport.com and how to read her credit score. Once she received it, she noticed multiple errors in the file. She also noticed that her credit score was very low. After looking through it, Patty was able to see what was damaging her credit and keeping her score down. She was also able to take action to fix it. The moral of the story is education is power. If Patty had not followed my suggestion, her credit report, and credit score would still be damaged.

TAKE ACTION!

Consumers move throughout life without understanding what type of impact their credit reports can have on their financial well-being. The information in your credit report can allow you to enjoy some of the finest things in life, or it can also make your life a struggle. For example, if you decide to give up on paying your bills, you could have difficulty getting a loan or an apartment, your insurance rates could go up, your marriage or relationship could suffer, and you could be denied employment. It's important to take responsibility, pay your bills on time, and understand the importance of credit reports. Take time to become familiar with the credit agencies that keep tabs on your payment history. These actions could produce great financial success. With good credit, banks and credit card companies will knock down your door trying to get your business. You would be able to qualify for the best interest rates when it comes to a credit card, car, bank loan, or home loan. You'll be able to take the trip that you have been waiting for, and your job opportunities will increase all because you took steps to improve your credit report.

What is a credit report and why is it important?

Your credit report is a snapshot of your payment history. It details when you applied for credit, how many positive and negative accounts you have, who viewed your credit report, and all of your personal information. Reviewing your credit report every four to six months gives you a chance to check for identity theft, inaccurate accounts, and incorrect information. It allows you to manage your financial situation before applying for a credit card, auto loan, bank loan, mortgage loan, employment, or insurance. For example, if you check your credit and notice that there were a few negative items on your report, you will have a chance to fix those items before applying for credit. By doing this, you avoid embarrassment and several inquiries, which lowers your credit score.

How does bad information get on my credit report?

Every month, the creditors and collection agencies that you have accounts with will report positive and negative information to the credit bureaus through a computer tape monitoring system that is updated regularly. The credit bureaus then turn around and update the information. A third-party company normally passes public record information onto the credit bureaus.

When does negative information come off my credit report?

Each negative item has a federal statute of limitation on when it must drop off your credit report. Once the statute of limitation has expired, the item must be deleted from your credit report according to the Fair Credit Reporting Act. The statute of limitation starts 180 days from the date the account became delinquent.

Federal Statute of Limitations

Late payments:

Once you become more than 30 days late on any of your bills, the financial institution that you hold the loan with will disclose your late status to the credit bureau. You can be reported as either 30, 60, or 90 days late, and by law, the late marks will remain on your credit report for seven years.

Inquiries:

Whenever you apply for a credit card or a loan, your credit report is checked, which results in a hard inquiry. These inquiries could damage your credit score if you have more than six in two months. They can also stay on your credit report for up to two years.

Charge offs:

These are debts that the creditor felt that they could not collect on anymore after 180 days, so they charged them off as a bad debt. However, the creditor can still sell the account to a third-party collector for collection purposes.

Judgments:

If a creditor takes you to court and sues for a judgment, this destructive item will be placed on your credit report. The courts issue judgments that can stay on your credit report for up to seven years, but it can be renewed until it is paid or until it reaches the 20-year mark. **See appendix for your state statute of limitation on judgments.**

Child support:

If you stop making child support payments, it becomes part of your public record and will therefore show up on your credit report. This negative mark can stay on your report for up to seven years.

Foreclosure/Repossession:

Foreclosures take place when you default on your home mortgage and the bank takes the house back. Repossession is when you can no longer pay your car note, and the lender confiscates the vehicle without your permission. Both create negative marks that will remain on your credit report for seven years.

Tax liens:

Tax liens are public records that will find their way into your credit report if you default on your tax liability with the IRS.

Paid tax liens will stay on your credit report for seven years, but while owed, they can remain on your record forever.

Collection:

If you see an old account on your credit report under the collection trade line, this is a bill that was sold or assigned to a collection agency. It was passed onto the collector from your original creditor because you refused to pay. These debts can legally stay on your credit report for up to seven years, but you cannot be sued for it after the state statute of limitation has expired. **See appendix for the state statute of limitation on revolving accounts.**

Bankruptcies:

Your credit report will list the date you filed for bankruptcy and the time it was discharged. A Chapter 7 bankruptcy can remain on your credit report for ten years, and a Chapter 13 bankruptcy will remain on your credit report for seven years.

Who uses the information in my credit report?

Banks, creditors, car dealers, mortgage brokers, and any other lending institutions use your credit report to determine if you are credit worthy of a loan. Collection agencies use the information in your credit report to track your location and see what other debts you owe. Insurance companies run your credit report to determine your insurance risk, and employment agencies view your report for employment considerations.

Tell me how to get my credit reports.

Currently, there are three main credit bureaus, Equifax, Experian and Trans Union. You should request your credit report from all three of these agencies. Your information is also available for free from each credit bureau every 12 months. Another option for obtaining personal credit reports is to get a three-in-one report. With this report, you get all three of your credit reports merged into one. If you want a three-in-one credit report, you have to buy it or subscribe to a credit monitoring service.

A good starting point for reviewing your credit history and information is The Annual Credit Report, a service sponsored by the three leading credit bureaus and authorized by the Federal Trade Commission. By using the Annual Credit Report website, you can see all three of your credit reports instantly as this service is offered to you for free once a year.

How do I get my credit report online?

You can get your credit report by logging onto Annualcreditreport.com. Once there, select "Get Your Free Credit Report" and fill out the subsequent form. You will be prompted for basic information, as well as a few questions regarding your accounts. After you have typed in the security code, you will be prompted to select a credit bureau to retrieve your credit report.

How do I get my reports by mail?

Also on Annualcreditreport.com is the option to request your reports by mail. Simply click on the link titled "Getting Your Credit Reports By Mail" and print out the form. Aside from basic information, you will need a copy of your license and a utility bill in order to fill out the form. While completing the form, make sure to use a black or blue pen. Once finished, send the form to Annual Credit Report Request Service, P.O. Box 105281, Atlanta, GA 30348-5281.

How do I request my free credit reports by phone?

Another option is to call the Annual Credit Report at 1-877-322-8228 and follow the automated voice prompts to order your credit reports. You can request one report, or all three. When you call, the automated system will ask you for personal information like your social security number, date of birth, full name, and your current and previous address. These actions are taken to prevent identity theft. Once your request is in, your reports will be mailed out to you within 15 days.

Are there other ways of obtaining my report for free?

According to federal law, you are entitled to an additional free report if you experience the following:

- If you are denied credit, insurance, or employment. (You then must request for your credit report within 60 days from being denied. Write to the credit bureaus and let them know that you were denied credit and that you would like a free credit report.)

- You're unemployed and plan to search for a job within 60 days

- If you are on welfare, or a victim of identity theft

- If the bank or a credit card company charges you higher rates or fees, and their decision was based on your credit report

- If there was a negative change in your credit limit or the collection agency tells you that they have reported adverse information on your credit report

What are the benefits of a three-in-one credit report?

- You can request a three-in-one report rather than dealing with each credit bureau individually

- In this report, all three credit reports are merged into one

- You can compare account information from all three bureaus

- There is less paper to deal with

- You are at one website versus three

What is the cost for a three-in-one report?

As of today, many companies offer three-in-one reports, but I recommend you stay with the three major agencies, Equifax, Trans Union, and Experian. Costs for these reports vary, and may change if you decide to get a credit score with your order.

What is the cost to obtain my credit report?

If you want to see your credit report more often than every 12 months, you can order them directly from the credit bureaus or subscribe to a monitoring service. With this service, you can get updated reports once a month for an annual or monthly fee. The price for the credit report varies from state to state, but it could cost you from $8.00 to $9.50.

You can purchase your credit report online, by mail, or by telephone from all three credit bureaus. Another way to track your credit report is by requesting one every four months instead of once per year. If you order your reports by mail, contact the credit bureaus and ask them what information is needed to get a copy of your credit report?

Send your request to:

Experian, NCAC, P.O. BOX 9701, ALLEN, TX 75013
www.experian.com   888-397-3742

Equifax, P.O. BOX 105518, ATLANTA, GA 30348
www.equifax.com   800-685-1111

Trans Union, P.O. BOX 2000, CHESTER, PA 19022
www.transunion.com   800-916-8800

What is Credit Monitoring?

Credit monitoring is a service offered by the main credit bureaus and other organizations. For a monthly fee, the companies will do the following:

- Pull your credit reports and scores for you every month
- Give you unlimited access to your reports
- Offer free credit management education
- Provide identity theft programs for your protection
- Monitor your credit report for activity
- Notify you (via email or phone) of any changes in your report
- Offer you the opportunity to review your report for any unauthorized accounts or activity

What information is in my credit report?

Every credit report looks slightly different, but it contains the same information about you and your accounts. Credit cards, car loans, and mortgage loans in your report are called trade lines. The consumer credit report starts with a summary of facts and your report number. The following is a list of critical information that you should pay attention to on your credit reports:

Cover Page:

When you first get your credit report, the cover page will have your name, report date, report number, and address of the credit bureaus.

Creditor/Collection Agency Name:

Here, the creditor or the collection agency will list their name and address, but no phone number is included. A partial number of your account will be listed also to protect you from identity theft.

Type and Responsibility:

This is the type of loan you have and who is responsible for the loan.

Date Open and Date of Status:

This is the date your account was opened and when the creditor first reported payment information about you to the credit bureau.

Reported Since and Last Reported:

This is the date the creditor first reported your payment history, as well as the last date they reported your status.

Terms and Monthly Payment:

This is how long you are contracted to pay the debt and how much you pay per month.

Credit Limit/Original Amount:

This area tells you how much your credit limit was when you first got the account.

Recent Balance and High Balance:

In this area, the credit report displays your most recent balance from your account and the highest balance you ever had with the trade line.

Status and Account History:

This section shows if you are current on your bills or if the account was closed or paid. Furthermore, it also displays your payment history.

Comments:

In this part of the report, the creditor will comment on whether the consumer closed the account or the lending institution closed the account.

History of Your Accounts:

This area will display your entire paying history since you opened the account, and each one of your accounts will be listed in this section.

Record of Request for Your Credit History:

In this section, you can see who requested to evaluate your credit report. Most companies looking at your information are your current creditor and collection agency. Under the shared inquiry area, which is in this section as well, will display companies that are trying to offer you pre-approved credit applications.

Personal Information:

Here, you will find your name, address, date of birth, telephone number, spouse name/co-applicant, and your employer's name. No social security number will be listed.

Public Records:

This section displays public record information like bankruptcies, judgments, tax liens, civil lawsuits, and overdue child support payments.

The remaining portion of your credit report contains addresses of companies that requested your credit report.

What are credit bureaus?

The three main credit bureaus are Equifax, Experian, and Trans Union. These organizations are part of a billion dollar industry, and they manage various databases that banks and credit cards companies subscribe to regularly. The credit bureaus maintain financial records and payment histories for over 100 million consumers. The credit bureaus sell consumer information to financial institutions. The Fair Credit Reporting Act (FCRA) heavily regulates the credit bureau.

Tell me about the fourth Credit Bureau: Innovis.

CBC companies developed a new credit bureau called Innovis. This credit agency is still trying to make its mark in the market of credit reports. If you pulled your information right now, it would not be as complete as the three main credit bureaus. Innovis does not offer credit reports for a fee; however, it is regulated by the FCRA, so if you request a credit report, they must send it to you.

Please write to Innovis at the address listed below:

Innovis Data Solutions
950 Threadneedle, Suite 200
Houston TX 77079-2903

What is ChexSystems?

If you have ever written fraudulent checks or failed to pay an outstanding balance with your bank, then you have probably been reported to ChexSystems. This business is just like the credit reporting agencies except that ChexSystems keeps track of customers who have written worthless checks.

In addition, ChexSystems tracks customers who fail to pay their debts to banks. For example, if you go to the bank and try to open a checking account, the bank will run your name and social security number through ChexSystems to determine whether you currently owe money to the bank, or whether you have ever written fraudulent checks. In such cases, your checking account may be denied.

To confirm your free ChexSystem report, go to www.consumerdebit.com. If you have a poor ChexSystems history, you still have the opportunity to consult with various banks to see if they offer the second chance program. In this program, you will have to attend a mandatory money management class, and you will be given a restricted account. During this probationary period, you cannot bounce checks or accumulate overdraft fees. If you fail to follow the strict guidelines, you can lose your checking account. If you choose not to go with a traditional bank, here is a list of non-ChexSystems banks:

www.cardreport.com/dirs/non-chexsystems-banks.html
http://chexsys.tripod.com/goodbanks.html
http://chexvictims.com/cs/

Key points to remember

- Get a copy of your credit report from annualcreditreport.com
- Order your credit score
- Get a copy of your ChexSystems report
- Request your report from the fourth credit bureaus Innovis
- Sign up for a credit monitoring service

CHAPTER 2:

The Dispute Process

Max's Story

While I was at the doctor having my back adjusted, Max came up to me and said, "I heard that you help people repair their credit." I said, "Yes, do you need help?" "Yes," he said shyly, "but I don't know whether you can help me." "I can help anyone with bad credit, Max." He went onto say that he had 16 charge offs on his credit report. I told him it shouldn't be a problem but that I would like to see a copy of his report. Days later, Max handed me his credit report, and sure enough there were 16 negative marks. I told him that I would draft a dispute letter to question six of the negative trade lines that do not belong to him. Max then stated, "How can you get those off my credit report?" I told Max that the law allows him to challenge the accuracy of any negative accounts on his report, so I prepared a letter and emailed it to him. He mailed the letters to the credit bureaus and waited for a response. When Max received his credit reports thirty days later, all six items were deleted. The moral of the story is that knowledge is power, and if Max had never approached me, those opposed marks would still be on his credit report.

TAKE ACTION NOW!

Using the dispute process to remove negative items off of your credit report can be time-consuming and frustrating. Nevertheless, it is one of the best ways to get negative information off of your credit report. Starting with the basic dispute process is quite often the fastest and most effective way of getting incorrect items off of your credit report. Now that you have your credit reports in front of you, make sure to check the personal information section and check that all entries are correct. Check your name, date of birth, present, and past address, current and past employer, and social security number. After you have verified your basic information, you should scan all three reports and circle or highlight any errors you find. Scroll down each report and check for any errors or discrepancies regarding accounts, or inquiries. Here are some important red flags to look for:

Discrepancies regarding accounts and inquiries

- Unauthorized users
- Customers listed as deceased
- Former spouse name
- Negative accounts from your divorce
- Negative co-signed accounts
- Unauthorized inquires
- Illegally re-aged collection accounts (which report an incorrect last date of activity)
- Foreclosure attempts
- Consumer credit counseling loan indications

Discrepancies regarding balances and accounts

- Balances incorrect
- Credit limits listed incorrectly

- Duplicate collections
- Accounts listed incorrectly
- Credit lines not listed
- Paid accounts still showing that you owe
- Closed accounts shown open
- Closed accounts should say closed by consumer and not closed by the creditor

Discrepancies regarding negative trade lines

- Late payments, 30, 90, and 120 days
- Collections
- Charge offs
- Tax liens
- Judgments
- Debt consolidation marks
- Bankruptcies not saying withdrawn or dismissed
- Repossession indication when it should say voluntary surrendered

Ok, I'm finished scanning my report, what's next?

Now, before you start trying to repair your credit report, let me tell you what the law says about challenging negative items on your report.

The Fair Credit Reporting Act regulates how the credit bureaus handle your credit report under § 611. For procedures in cases of disputed accuracy [15 U.S.C. § 1681i], the law states that if you dispute the accuracy of any item or data in your credit reports, the credit bureau shall conduct a reasonable investigation within 30 days to determine if the challenged item is correct.

After the 30 days have expired, if the credit bureau has not verified or completed the investigation, the disputed item must be deleted. There you go, that is the law, and you will use it to start your dispute process. Now we need to get your filing system set up first, so you can establish proof just in case you have to sue the credit bureau or collection agency in court.

How do I set up my filing system?

First, go to the office supply store and buy a box of fresh filing folders with labels to keep track of the three credit bureaus. Once you have the folders, label them by the credit bureau's name, and start filing your correspondence with each credit bureau when you begin your disputes.

For example, if you send off a dispute letter to Equifax, place that letter along with your certified return receipt in the Equifax folder. Once you receive a response, you should record their answer in the Equifax folder and record it in the dispute tracking form according to its date. **See appendix for a sample dispute tracking form.**

Before you send your first letter, make sure to properly fill out the dispute tracking form. In addition, you can keep track of how much time and money you spent on your efforts to clean up your credit report. If you have taken time off from work to do credit repair related issues, keep track of the date and amount of time taken off. You should also keep track of names, dates and phone calls made to and from the credit bureaus. A good reason to do this is in preparation for a lawsuit against the credit bureau for failing to investigate your disputed items. Plenty of documentation will be needed in order to have sufficient evidence to win your lawsuit.

I have the system in place?

There are three powerful ways you can fix your credit report. First, you can use the standard dispute procedure to remove trade lines. Second, settle your debt with creditors for a complete deletion of negative information. And third, sue the creditor bureaus to remove harmful information from your credit report.

How do I begin the basic dispute process?

You can begin by writing the credit bureau to dispute any negative items you think are incorrect. With this method, you can get results if you keep at it.

How about repairing my credit with settlement techniques?

Settlement techniques are another powerful way to have negative items removed from your report. If you pay the outstanding balance, you can negotiate with creditors or the collection agency to have the harmful item removed. Before using this strategy, you must make sure you have the money ready to send.

What about suing the credit bureau method?

This method will get the results you need most of the time, as some credit bureaus will not reinvestigate your dispute. If this is the case, you may have no other choice but to sue the credit bureaus for violation of the FCRA. During the lawsuit, you can sue for injunctive relief (stopping the credit reporting agency from reporting negative information on your report). You can find more details about suing credit bureaus in chapter eleven.

Where should I start?

You want to start with the dispute process. You can write your own dispute letter or use the 12-step dispute plan. If you decide to write the letters, you must include your full name, date of birth, address, social security number, the items you're disputing, the reason you are disputing them and your signature at the bottom. Before sending out your first letter, please review the dispute key points.

Dispute key points to remember:

- Use a polite and friendly tone in the first letter.

- When disputing, only challenge two to three items at a time, so that the credit bureau does not think you are abusing the system. If they feel that your disputes are frivolous (unworthy of serious attention), they will not want to initiate the investigation.

- Dispute the easiest items first, then moved to the hardest one.

- Never use the phone, web services, or the letter dispute forms that come with the credit report because you have limited space to challenge your negative items.

- In your disputes, use vague phrases like, "I don't remember this account being mine."

- Major negative items like bankruptcies, repossessions and foreclosures should be disputed on the bases of a complete deletion.

- Become more threatening with each dispute.

- Send disputes during the holidays like Thanksgiving and Christmas. During this time the credit bureaus are busy with creditors making it hard for them to meet the 30-day deadline.

- Negative items remaining on your credit report should be challenged over and over until they are removed.

- Set reminders on your computer for 40 days, so that you can keep track of when you sent out your first dispute letter.

- After you receive your response back from the credit bureau, wait five days before sending out your second dispute letter.

- Repeat the basic dispute method three times before moving to the other strategies.

- Dispute different items with each credit bureau to see which negative listing comes off first.

What are the easiest items to dispute first?

- Outdated accounts

- Late payments over three years on closed accounts

- Accounts that were late but are now paid off

- Charge offs and settled accounts

- Authorized user accounts

- Accounts that do not belong to you

What are the hardest items to challenge?

- A fresh Chapter 7 and 13 bankruptcy
- New foreclosures and repossessions
- Unpaid tax liens and judgments
- Recent charge offs and new collections
- New late payments 30, 90, 120 days and child support

What reasons can I use for my dispute?

- The account is not yours
- You have no record of being late
- The trademark displays the wrong amount
- Incorrect account number
- Accounts are unverifiable
- The original creditor is wrong
- Inaccurate charge off date
- Date of last activity is wrong
- Credit limit is incorrect
- Status is wrong
- High credit is wrong
- Charge off amount is wrong
- Wrong balance
- The accounts have inconsistencies
- Items are questionable or misleading
- The accounts are erroneous

- Outdated

- Inaccurate or incorrect

How do I use the dispute letters?

When using dispute letters, enter the information in the letter as directed. Make sure you put your report number at the top of the letter. Within the dispute letter, enter the reason for your dispute. You can find various valid reasons to dispute in the reason section indicated above. Retype and print out the first dispute letter and then sign it. Make a copy of each credit report with the negative items circled and send it with your first dispute letter. Include any proof that will help validate your claim, for example, receipts stating that the item was paid.

Include a copy of your driver's license and a recent utility bill that displays your name and address, as the credit bureau needs this information to verify your identity. Every time you send a dispute letter, send a copy of your credit report with the negative items highlighted. Mail your letters certified mail with a return receipt to establish a paper trail just in case you have to sue the credit bureau for failing to investigate your disputes. Send your letters to the following credit bureaus listed below.

Experian
NCAC PO BOX 9701
ALLEN TX, 75013

Equifax
PO BOX 105518
ATLANTA GA, 30348

Trans Union
PO BOX 2000
CHESTER PA, 19022

Key points to remember

- Set up your filing system
- Scan your credit reports for errors
- Follow the key points
- Send all letters certified mail with return receipts
- Start the dispute process

DISPUTE LETTERS IN MICROSOFT WORD FORMAT AVAILABLE AT

HIDDENCREDITREPAIRSECRETS.COM

The 12-STEP DISPUTE PLAN

Dispute letter one:

After 30 days, you should hear back from the credit bureau. Your results will state that either your item has been deleted or has been verified and remains with no change. If the results are that your disputed item has been deleted, start from the beginning of the 12-step dispute plan and begin challenging other negative items that you believe are incorrect.

Your Full name:
Your Address:
Your Date of Birth:
Your Social Security number:
Report Number:
Date:

Dear Credit Bureau
I'm writing to let you know that your company is reporting inaccurate credit information on my credit report. The FCRA ensures that bureaus report only 100% accurate information. Therefore, I would like for the following information to be investigated.
Account one:
Account two:
Account three:
Please delete this misleading information, and supply me with a corrected credit report within 30 days.

Sincerely,
Print your name here.
Sign your name here.

Dispute letter two:

If there is no change in your credit report, then you should send dispute letter two with more aggressive language. For example, phrases like "I'm distressed at the fact" or "this negative item is damaging on my credit report" tend to get the attention of the credit bureaus. You will simply repeat your same reasoning as to why you are disputing the negative item. This letter and all subsequent letters should be sent certified mail with a return receipt.

Your Full name:
Your Address:
Your Date of Birth:
Your Social Security number:
Report Number:
Date:

Dear Credit Bureau
I'm stressed at the fact that your company is reporting incorrect information on my credit report. Please reinvestigate the accounts listed below according to the FCRA.
Account one:
Account two:
Account three:
Please delete this misleading information, and supply me with a corrected credit report within 30 days.

Sincerely,
Print your name here.
Sign your name here.

Dispute letter three:

After 30 days, you should hear back from the credit bureau. Again, your results will state that your item has either been deleted or has been verified and remains with no change. If the results are that the following items have been deleted, then start from the beginning of the 12-step dispute plan and begin challenging other negative items that you believe are incorrect. If there is no change, send dispute letter three asking the credit bureau to provide you with their verification procedures (the procedures they took to verify the negative item). You are asking the credit bureau to send you documentation on how they are verifying your debts. Within this letter, repeat your dispute but this time change up your reasoning to give the credit bureau a new reason to investigate the dispute.

Your Full name:
Your Address:
Your Date of Birth:
Your Social Security number:
Report Number:
Date:

Dear Credit Bureau
I'm requesting that you provide me with the description of the procedures used to investigate my trade lines in compliance with the FCRA, section 611, part B, subsection iii. As a matter of convenience, I'm resubmitting my request to correct my credit report.
Account one:
Account two:
Account three:
Please delete this misleading information, and supply me with a corrected credit report within 30 days.

Sincerely,
Print your name here.
Sign your name here.

Dispute letter four:

After 30 days, you should hear back from the credit bureau. Your results will state that your item has either been deleted or verified and remains with no change. If the results are that the following items have been deleted, then start from the beginning of the 12-step dispute plan and begin challenging other negative items that you believe are incorrect. If there is no change, send dispute letter four threatening to file a complaint with the Federal Trade Commission. The FTC regulates the credit bureaus, and if they receive enough complaints from consumers, it may result into a lawsuit against the credit bureaus. Within this letter, repeat your dispute so that the credit bureau will reinvestigate the matter.

Your Full name:
Your Address:
Your Date of Birth:
Your Social Security number:
Report Number:
Date:

Dear Credit Bureau
This is the fourth letter I'm writing about incorrect information on my credit report, and I'm starting to become emotionally stressed at the fact that your company is not fixing the problem. According to 15 USC section 1681i of the FCRA, I demand that these items be reinvestigated and deleted from my record.
Account one:
Account two:
Account three:
Please delete this misleading information, and supply me with a corrected credit report within 30 days. If for some reason, your company fails to investigate, I will have no other choice but to file a complaint with the FTC.

Sincerely,
Print your name here.
Sign your name here.

Dispute letter five:

After 30 days, you should hear back from the credit bureau. Your results will state that either your item has either been deleted or has been verified and remains with no change. If the results are that the following items have been deleted, then start from the beginning of the 12-step dispute plan and begin challenging other negative items that you believe are incorrect. If there is no change, send dispute letter five stating that you have filed a complaint with the FTC. Also send them a copy of your complaint. Within this letter, repeat your dispute, but this time change up your reasoning to give the credit bureau a new reason to investigate the dispute.

Your Full name:
Your Address:
Your Date of Birth:
Your Social Security number:
Report Number:
Date:

Dear Credit Bureau
I'm writing for the fifth time with a formal request to correct inaccurate information listed in my credit report. In the last letter, I advised your company that a complaint would be filed with the FTC if the incorrect items were not investigated. Please be aware that the complaint was indeed filed (see the attached complaint). In accordance with the FCRA, I request that your company investigate my disputes.
Account one:
Account two:
Account three:
Please delete this misleading information, and supply me with a corrected credit report within 30 days.

Sincerely,
Print your name here.
Sign your name here.

Dispute letter six:

After 30 days, you should hear back from the credit bureau. Your results will state that either your item has either been deleted or has been verified and remains with no change. If the results are that the following items have been deleted then start from the beginning of the 12-step dispute plan and begin challenging other negative items that you believe are incorrect. If there is no change, send dispute letter six threatening to file a complaint with the attorney general's office. Credit bureau hate to hear the attorney general's office mentioned because once they get involved, the negative marks must be investigated. Within this letter, repeat your dispute so that the credit bureau will reinvestigate the matter.

Your Full name:
Your Address:
Your Date of Birth:
Your Social Security number:
Report Number:
Date:

Dear Credit Bureau
This is the sixth letter that I am sending after reviewing my credit report. I have identified the following problems:
Account one:
Account two:
Account three:
Please delete this misleading information, and supply me with a corrected credit report within 30 days. If no investigation takes place, I will be forced to file a complaint with the attorney general's office.

Sincerely,
Print your name here.
Sign your name here.

Dispute letter seven:

After 30 days, you should hear back from the credit bureau. Your results will state that either your item has been deleted or has been verified and remains with no change. If the results are that the following items have been deleted, then start from the beginning of the 12-step dispute plan and begin challenge other negative items that you believe are incorrect. If there is no change, send dispute letter seven advising the credit bureau that you have filed a complaint with the attorney general's office. At this point, the attorney general's office will notify you that they have received your complaint and will try to contact the credit bureau. Once a letter from the attorney general's office goes out to the credit bureau, they will stop ignoring your request and start a new investigation. Within this letter, repeat your dispute so that the credit bureau will reinvestigate the matter.

Your Full name:
Your Address:
Your Date of Birth:
Your Social Security number:
Report Number:
Date:

Dear Credit Bureau
After checking my credit report, I noticed the following trade lines are still incomplete. Please see the attached credit report for highlighted errors. By the provision of the FCRA, I demand that the misleading items be investigated and removed from my file.
Account one:
Account two:
Account three:
Please delete this misleading information, and supply me with a corrected credit report within 30 days. In my last letter, I advised that I would file a complaint with the attorney general's office. Please see the attached complaint to this letter.

Sincerely,
Print your name here.
Sign your name here.

Dispute letter eight:

After 30 days, you should hear back from the credit bureau. Your results will state that either your item has been deleted or has been verified and remains with no change. Again, if the results are that the following items have been deleted, then start from the beginning of the 12-step dispute plan and begin challenging other negative items that you believe are incorrect. If there is no change, send dispute letter eight advising the credit bureau that you will file a complaint with your state senators. This technique is powerful because state senators have much power and they want to know how consumers are being treated by the credit bureaus. Within this letter, repeat your dispute, but this time change up your reasoning to give the credit bureau a new reason to investigate the dispute.

Your Full name:
Your Address:
Your Date of Birth:
Your Social Security number:
Report Number:
Date:

Dear Credit Bureau
This is the eighth letter that I have sent regarding misleading information being reported on my credit report. I demand that these inaccurate items be removed to reflect my true credit history.
Account one:
Account two:
Account three:
Please delete this misleading information, and supply me with a corrected credit report within 30 days. If for some reason, your company chose not to investigate, I will have no other choice but to file a complaint with my state senators.

Sincerely,
Print your name here.
Sign your name here.

Dispute letter nine:

After 30 days, you should hear back from the credit bureau, and your results will state that either your item has been deleted or verified and remains with no change. If the results are that the following items have been deleted, then start from the beginning of the 12-step dispute plan and begin challenging other negative items that you believe are incorrect. If there is no change, send dispute letter nine advising the credit bureau that you have filed a complaint with your state senator. Before you send this letter, wait for a response from your state senator's office and send a copy along with your letter. Within this letter, repeat your dispute so that the credit bureau will reinvestigate the matter.

Your Full name:
Your Address:
Your Date of Birth:
Your Social Security number:
Report Number:
Date:

Dear Credit Bureau
Recently, I reviewed my credit report and noticed that the same negative trade lines are being reported. For the ninth time, I'm demanding that your company reinvestigate my disputes. The problems with these accounts are as follows:
Account one:
Account two:
Account three:
Please delete this misleading information, and supply me with a corrected credit report within 30 days. In my last letter, I advised your company that I would file a complaint with my state senators if an investigation did not take place, so I did. See the complaint form attached to this letter.

Sincerely,
Print your name here.
Sign your name here.

Dispute letter ten:

After 30 days, you should hear back from the credit bureau. Your results will state that either your item has been deleted or has been verified and remains with no change. If the results are that the following items have been deleted, then start from the beginning of the 12-step dispute plan and begin challenging other negative items that you believe are incorrect. Send dispute letter ten advising the credit bureau that you have filed a complaint with the Federal Deposit Insurance Corporation, Comptroller of the Currency Federal Reserve System. These committees are interested in individual issues and problems in the credit-reporting field. Wait to you get a response from Federal Deposit Insurance Corporation, Comptroller of the Currency Federal Reserve System, and then attach the letters to your dispute. Within this letter, repeat your dispute, but this time, reorganize your presentation to give the credit bureau a new reason to investigate the dispute.

Your Full name:
Your Address:
Your Date of Birth:
Your Social Security number:
Report Number:
Date:
Dear Credit Bureau
It seems to me that you are refusing to investigate my disputes, which is a violation of the FCRA. I have written nine letters disputing the fact that the trade lines listed below are inaccurate, but your company refused to investigate. Because of your noncompliance, I have filed a complaint with the Federal Deposit Insurance Corporation, Comptroller of the Currency Federal Reserve System. For the tenth time, please investigate my disputes.
Account one:
Account two:
Account three:
Please delete this misleading information, and supply me with a corrected credit report within 30 days.

Sincerely,
Print your name here.
Sign your name here.

Dispute letter eleven:

After 30 days, you should hear back from the credit bureau, and your results will either state that your item has been deleted or verified and remains with no change. If the results are, the following items have been deleted. Then start from the beginning of the 12-step dispute plan and begin challenging other negative items that you believe is incorrect. Send dispute letter eleven advising the credit bureau that you will seek legal advice if this matter is not resolved. Within this letter, repeat your dispute so that the credit bureau will reinvestigate the matter.

Your Full name:
Your Address:
Your Date of Birth:
Your Social Security number:
Report Number:
Date:

Dear Credit bureau,
It's now my 11th letter, and yet you still refused to investigate the misleading accounts listed below. Because of your failures, I have lost the opportunity to get better interest rates and suffered damaged to my credit worthiness and character. Therefore, I have to seek legal advice if this matter is not fixed, so please reinvestigate the following accounts:
Account one:
Account two:
Account three:
Please delete this misleading information, and supply me with a corrected credit report within 30 days.

Sincerely,
Print your name here.
Sign your name here.

Dispute letter twelve:

After 30 days, you should hear back from the credit bureau, and your results will either state that your item has been deleted or verified and remains with no change. If the results are, the following items have been deleted. Then start from the beginning of the 12-step dispute plan and begin challenging other negative items that you believe is incorrect. Send dispute letter twelve advising the credit bureau that you will sue them for noncompliance. From then, you must hire a lawyer to sue or you can sue by yourself in small claims court. Within this letter, repeat your dispute so that the credit bureau will reinvestigate the matter.

Your Full name:
Your Address:
Your Date of Birth:
Your Social Security number:
Report Number:
Date:

Dear Credit Bureau
This will be my last letter that I will send regarding the inaccurate accounts listed. After the 11th letter, your company is still failing to comply with the FCRA. As of right now, if the negative items listed below are not reinvestigated and fixed, I will sue your company for willful non-compliance and $5,000 for each item you refuse to investigate. I will re-list the problem accounts.
Account one:
Account two:
Account three:
Please delete this misleading information, and supply me with a corrected credit report within 30 days.

Sincerely,
Print your name here.
Sign your name here.

Chapter 3:

When the Credit Bureaus Won't Fix My Credit Report

Mark's Story

While I was in the process of repairing my credit, there was one account on my report that did not belong to me, but TransUnion continued to verify it anyway. After sending three dispute letters, TransUnion sent me a letter stating that my disputes were frivolous. I thought to myself, how could TransUnion verify a debt that is not really mine.

Let me tell you what happened. When I sent the first dispute letter, TransUnion contacted the creditor for verification. The creditor mistakenly verified that it was my debt, and as a result, the debt was verified in TransUnion's computer. Despite consecutive disputes, the credit bureau never contacted the original creditor again, even when I re-explained the dispute.

TransUnion simply looked into their files to see that the disputed account was verified. They failed to investigate the matter further, despite its negative affect on my credit. With my knowledge on the laws of credit repair, I knew that Trans Union and the creditor were violating the Fair Credit Reporting Act, so I filed a complaint with the attorney general's office in the credit bureaus and the creditor's state. After a few weeks, I received a letter from both attorney generals stating that they were forwarding my complaint to the credit bureau and the creditor. A month later, I received an updated credit report from TransUnion with the item deleted. The moral of the story is education is power. Through knowing which office to direct a complaint to in order to force the hand of an uncooperative creditor, I was able to remove a negative item from my file.

TAKE ACTION NOW!

For years, credit bureaus have taken advantage of consumers who lack knowledge in the credit repair process by failing to investigate legitimate disputes. Because the credit bureaus business is driven by profits, they tend to take the word of the creditor when it comes to verifying a negative account. It does not matter if the account is incorrect, the credit bureau will still state that the damaging item is verified as yours. This, in return, will continue to damage your credit worthiness. To keep the credit bureaus objective, there are various organizations to which you as a consumer can contact in order to keep the credit bureaus in line.

There was no change in my credit report, now what?

After the 30 day investigation period is over, the credit bureau will send you an updated credit report indicating the changes if any. They will say one of the following:

- The item has been verified and no change has been made.
- They feel that you are working with a credit repair company.
- They consider the dispute frivolous.

If your disputed items come back verified, draft a new dispute letter and use one of the following techniques to prompt a new investigation:

Verification method:

Ask the credit bureau for their method of verification using a standard dispute letter. Once you have been informed of the reasoning behind their rejection, you may develop a more fully formed picture of your credit history. With this new information, you can then repeat your complaint while bringing up different reasons for your dispute.

Wait period:

Wait 60 days and try again raising a different reason for your dispute. You can also change the tone of your letter by re-verbalizing and highlighting how the dispute has been the most damaging to you. Use phrases like "I have been terribly stressed," and "I am very worried about my credit worthiness being damaged" due to their failure to investigate your disputes.

Send Proof:

Send another dispute letter providing proof and sufficient documentation regarding why the negative mark should be removed. Write, with clarity and detail, explaining why the negative items are incorrect. This may especially be helpful if you have received a response asking for more information to continue the investigation.

Dispute the E-Oscar method:

With the Oscar system, the credit bureaus take your dispute and convert it into a two to three digit code. These codes can represent actions like "item not mine" or "item incorrect." The credit bureau then sends these codes to the creditor through the computer automated Oscar system for verification. The creditor will respond back with a code stating whether or not the item is correct.

Aside from disputing the negative item itself, you may also have to write to the credit bureaus disputing their use of the Oscar method. They are required to follow FCRA guidelines, and not the Oscar method, when verifying the accuracy of a disputed item.

Attach copies of other credit reports:

Advise the credit bureau that two of your credit reports from the other credit bureaus do not reflect this negative account, but on the disputed report, the negative item is still there. After you explain yourself, repeat your dispute and attach copies of the other two credit reports as proof.

Make the creditor prove that it's your debt:

Challenge the debt with the creditor by calling them up and asking for proof that you owe the debt. Proof meaning a copy of the original credit application or loan application with your signature. Moreover, ask them for your payment history showing that you were late on that particular day. If the creditor can't prove the adverse information reported, then they must delete it according to the FCRA. Give them 17 days to respond to your letter. If they do not provide a response, contact the attorney general's office in the creditor's state. You want to let them know that the creditor is reporting negative information on your credit report when they can't provide you with evidence. This is a violation of Federal law and is grounds for a lawsuit.

Let them know that you have grounds to sue them for $5,000 per disputed item they refuse to investigate. Once you have informed them, you can then repeat your dispute. By sending this letter to their legal department, you are more than likely to get a response.

Go straight to their legal department:

Address a letter to their legal department asking them why they have updated some inaccurate accounts but not others.

Also, request a copy of the completed verification form used and the contract information from the creditor who responded to the verification. You also want the creditor's name, title, and phone number, and a copy of the documents relied on as evidence of the debt.

Advise an attorney:

If necessary, let them know that you have contacted a lawyer and are considering a lawsuit for willful noncompliance (FCRA-616). This option should be considered once you have explored several of the previously listed alternatives. In the event that you file a lawsuit, you will need to have thorough documentation of your attempts to contact the bureau, dispute each negative mark, and explain your situation. Be sure to keep copies of each letter for your own records and orderliness as well.

Steps to take if the dispute has been deemed frivolous:

Write the credit bureau back and ask them to provide you with a reason on why they feel that your disputes are frivolous. In addition, ask them what they need you to do to continue the investigation. Listed below are some techniques you can use to prompt a new investigation in the event that your dispute has been deemed frivolous. **You can also see the appendix for sample response letters.**

Contact the manager:

Send your letter to the manager of the customer relations department. Once the letter goes there, they normally restart the dispute process because they may think that you are seeking legal advice.

Better Business Bureau:

File a complaint with your local Better Business Bureau and let the credit bureaus know that you have filed. The credit bureau, like any other business, aims to look good to potential customers and will avoid too many negative remarks against it.

Contact your state senators:

Let the credit bureau know that you plan to file a complaint with your state senator's office. Send copies of your complaint letter along with your dispute form to the credit bureau.

What organization should I complain to?

You can address multiple agencies as each agency has an interest in how the credit bureaus treat consumers. Here is the list of organizations you can send your letters to:

- The Federal Trade Commission
- The State Regulatory Agency
- Federal Deposit Insurance Corporation
- Comptroller of the Currency Federal Reserve System
- Credit and Insurance
- California Regulatory Agency Division of Consumer Complaints
- Bank Card Holders of America
- Call for Action, and the Office of the Attorney Generals

Include a copy of your complaint with your dispute letter to the credit bureaus.

What happens if the credit bureau does not respond?

According to the FCRA, the credit bureau has 30 days to investigate and return a response to you. If they fail to respond within the designated amount of time, they must delete the item in dispute. If they fail to respond, write them a second follow up letter demanding that they delete the item in question because they have failed to comply with FCRA guidelines. Remember to keep sufficient documentation of your correspondence. Include a copy of the first letter and a copy of the certified return receipt. If they still do not respond after your second letter, write a final letter advising them that they are in violation of FCRA. In addition, let them know that you will file a complaint with the Federal Trade Commission and Office of the Attorney General in order to seek legal advice. **See follow up letters in the appendix.**

Key points to remember

- Use the various methods to get the credit bureau to start a new investigation

- Employ advance techniques if you get a letter stating that your disputes are frivolous

- Send a second follow up letter when the credit bureau does not respond

Chapter 4:

Removing the "Eleven Killers" From My Credit Report

Rose's Story

Back in my working days, one of my co-workers was struggling with her bills. She would always ask me for advice on what she should do or what she should say to her creditors.

One day, she told me that she was thinking about filing for bankruptcy because of the overwhelming sum of her bills. She told me that she received a summons in the mail to show up in court to face a creditor. She was desperate and at her wits end. I explained to her that she needed to go to court to face the problem, and that she should plead hardship to the judge. By pleading hardship, she would have to bring proof that she could not pay the entire amount that the credit card company was asking for, but she would show that she was willing to make payments toward paying it off.

Rose did exactly that. She began by facing the hugeness of the problem, but also by explaining to those involved that she wanted to prove herself as a reliable, responsible individual. The judge ordered the creditor to accept her payment arrangement on her terms. By doing this, she avoided a judgment on her credit report, and prevented her wages from being garnished. The moral of the story is education is power. If Rose had not shown up in court like most people do, the creditor would have received a judgment by default allowing them to go after Rose's wages and damaging her credit reports.

TAKE ACTION!

The average American consumer is often overwhelmed by debt. And once accumulated, debt is not easy to get rid of. Nor is it an easy thing to face. Creditors and collection agencies understand and take advantage of this. The deeper into debt you get, the more money they collect. The only way to rid yourself of these outstanding debts is to fight them with education. You must understand the various options and laws that are in place to help you eliminate your debt and improve your financial picture. By doing this, it will give you hope that your situation can change.

Late payments

How can I avoid being delinquent on my account?

Being delinquent is where your payment is not received on the due date, and is therefore considered delinquent. Being late on your payments can drop your credit score by 50 points or more because your payment history makes up 35% of your credit score. To prevent you from getting behind, try applying some of the following helpful strategies.

- Have your online credit card company send you an automatic reminder.
- Set your calendar up to remind you seven days before your payments are due.
- Set your calendar up on your phone to alert you seven days before your due date.

- Set up automatic payment with your online banking company.

- Set up automatic withdraws through your credit card or financial company.

- If you follow these simple techniques, you will never miss a payment again.

What if I'm only a few days late on my payment?

Some credit card companies and lending institutions have grace periods, so if you are a few days late, you won't be charged a fee or be reported to the credit bureau. Even so, be warned, a lot of credit card companies do not have grace periods, so if you are behind one day, you will get hit with a high late fee. If you are in a special program that requires timely payments, this may ruin your chance to receive a credit increase. Check with your credit card company regarding their policies on grace periods.

What if I was 30 days late one or two times?

You will severely damage your credit score because your payment history counts for 35% of your credit score. Fico looks at the most recent payment activity. So if you were late two times within two years, your score will take a serious hit. According to Fico, negative information past two years does not count as much.

Can I use the good will letter to remove late payment?

Use this letter when you have late payments, and you are trying to get them removed from your credit report. The first step is to write the creditor with a polite letter. Say nice things about the company, for example what drew you to open a card with them in the first place or what you've enjoyed about their service. Then explain how your problems came about. Appeal to their good will while letting them know that something serious has happened and has caused you to fall behind in your payments. Let them know that you are up-to-date, and would like the late payment removed from your credit report. Thank them for taking the time to read your letter. **See a sample good will letter in the appendix.**

Collections

What is a collection account?

It's a negative trade line on your credit report that was reported by a collection agency. These accounts normally appear on your credit report because the consumer refused to pay a bill owed to a financial or other institution. Paid and unpaid collection accounts will stay on your credit report seven years from the date the account went delinquent with the original owner.

How do I remove a new unpaid collection on my credit report?

If the account is yours, and the collection is less than two years old, you can try the basic dispute strategies mentioned in chapter two. If you are unsuccessful in challenging it through the credit bureau, send a cease and desist letter (instructing the collection agency not to contact you in any form) to the collection agency and wait for the account to go back to the original creditor. When it's with the creditor, try to negotiate the debt for pennies on the dollar only if the creditor agrees to delete the negative item from your credit report. If they don't agree to delete the item, try to get a paid as agreed indication on your report. **See settlement techniques in chapter five.**

How do I get a paid collection off of my credit report?

If you want your credit score to go up and the paid collection is less than two years, try to get it deleted by using the basic dispute method. When you dispute a satisfied collection, most collectors will not respond to the creditor bureau when they try to validate the debt because the account is already paid, and they are too busy handling other unpaid accounts. The reason you want to remove the collection if it's less than two years is because negative accounts less than two years brings your score down further than accounts past two years. While disputing with the credit bureau, you can also send a good will letter to the creditor asking them to remove the collection from your credit report. Sometimes this method works if you word the letter right. Last, if you don't have the money to pay and no time or patience to dispute the item month after month, you can wait for the item to fall off of your credit report which is seven years from the date it went delinquent.

Charge offs

Can you tell me how to avoid a charge off?

When the bank can no longer collect on a debt, it writes of the account as a bad debt, which is called a charge off. Allowing your account to fall so far behind that it turns into a charge off will not only damage your credit score further, but also it will also cause you other financial problems.

- Ask the bank to suspend the late payments until you catch up.
- Ask the bank about hardship programs.
- Ask the bank to freeze your account until you can catch up with your payment.

- If you have the money, try to settle your debts for pennies on the dollar.

What happens if I'm approaching the 180-day deadline?

If you don't resolve your delinquent account before 180 days, the account will take one of the following courses:

- Charged off and the lender will take a tax write off. If the debt is more than $600, then the lender is required to send you a 1099-c with the amount charged off and report the charge off debt to the IRS. The IRS considers the charged off debt as a gain to you, therefore you must pay income taxes on it.
- Sell or assign your debt to a collection agency
- Assign the debt to their prepaid legal department for a possible lawsuit.

How do I deal with a charge off on my account?

Dispute the information inside of the charge off listing, for example, the date the account was open, the high balance, or the amount owed. If any of the information is incorrect, you have a good chance of getting it deleted by contacting the creditor and negotiating to have the adverse information removed. If you were not able to get the item removed, take the paid as agreed indication. After paying the debt, start your basic dispute method. During your dispute process, the negative item you just settled will be easy to come off because the creditor is already paid.

Even though the account is charged off, can the creditor still collect money owed?

Yes, just because the account is charged off does not mean the creditor can't come after you. They can still hire a third party collection agency to collect the debt from you.

Judgments

How do I avoid a money judgment on my credit report?

When the court orders one party to the lawsuit to pay the other party a certain amount of money. The amount of money awarded to the winner is called a money judgment. Try to avoid the debt from becoming a judgment by either settling the outstanding account or setting up a payment plan.

I just got a summons to appear in court for an old debt. What should I do?

If your income is low and you can't afford to settle the debt, go to court with a payment agreement in mind. Be sure to bring proof that you can't afford the full amount of the debt. This could include copies of your lease, utility bill, student loan payments and other documents. Since the judge has the power to force the creditor to enter a payment agreement, ask for a payment plan to avoid a judgment. In return, the creditor's attorney will request for a stipulation of judgment, which means that if you default on the agreement, the creditor's counsel can get a judgment entered without having to sue you.

I just pulled my credit report and noticed a judgment.

First, write down the court information listed under the judgment in your credit report, then contact the court and ask them to send you a copy of the judgment. Once you have a copy of the judgment, try any of the following techniques to remove it from your report.

- Try the basic dispute method to see whether the judgment will simply fall off.

- If you have no success with challenging negative items, you can settle them for 20-50 cents on the dollar and try for a deletion. If the creditor won't accept a complete deletion, request that your creditor list your account as "paid as agreed." From there you can begin the basic dispute process. Make sure you get a judgment satisfaction letter to send to the court advising them that the debt was paid. **See sample letter in the appendix.**

- You can make an agreement with the creditor's counsel to stand still for full payment of the debt. You can then file a motion (i.e. make a request) to have the judgment vacated based on a mistake such as a clerical error. Most likely, the attorney will not respond to your motion. As a result, the judgment will be vacated. Make sure you send the order to the credit bureaus for complete deletion.

- You can file a motion to have the judgment vacated (dismissed) based on a technicality, errors in the complaint, or the judgment has moved to another state, or the collection agency did not validate the debt. A technicality can be. You were not properly served or the statute of limitation has run out to collect the debt. You can find errors in the complaint like. The amount of the judgment was wrong. Your name is misspelled, or the date is incorrect.

- You can file a motion to have the judgment vacated based on discrepancies in the notice or any difficulties in obtaining it. For example, if you did not initially receive the notice, if the server left the notice on your doorstep or at an incorrect address, or if your spouse was served instead of you, you may be able to have the judgment vacated. Also, if the notice has the wrong district indicated, your name incorrectly listed, or if you were ill on the day of court, you may also be able to file a motion.

- If the judgment follows you to another state, you can dispute the interest by arguing that the collection agency did not validate your debt according to the FDCPA. By doing this, it can result to the judgment being vacated. **See sample motion to vacate the judgment in the appendix.**

How do I file a motion to have the judgment set aside?

Call the clerk and ask for the procedures on filing a motion to set aside a default judgment. After doing this, talk with a Prepaid Legal Attorney for assistance on taking the next step or to help you write the motion.

For a lawyer to help you with the motion, go to prepaidlegal.com and sign up for a membership. You can also check out www.examplemotion.com.

What can happen if I don't pay the judgment?

The judgment creditor (the person who owns the debt) can come after you by filing a court order directing you to appear in court to answer questions on why you have not paid the judgment. The judgment creditor can add enforcement costs to collect the judgment, add interest fees, force you to go to court and expose your assets, attach leans to your personal and real property, seize your car, access your bank account, and garnish your paycheck. They can force the sale of your property if the debt is a high amount. In addition, they can have your driver's license or professional license suspended if the judgment was from a motor vehicle accident or work pertaining to your career.

Can the judgment follow me if I move to another state?

Yes, your judgment creditor can register the judgment in the state you moved to. More than likely the creditor won't come after you, unless it's an attorney that has a law firm located in the state you moved to.

Can I appeal the judgment?

Yes, before the judgment creditor can collect, you have a short amount of time to appeal to the judge's decision. This strategy is good if you need more time to come up with the money.

How can I stop the judgment creditor from going after the equity in my home?

Protect your home against a force sale by using the homestead exemption. If you know that a creditor has obtained a judgment against you, go down to your local county recorder's office and file a declaration of homestead. This form lets the creditor know that you are claiming your home as a homestead. Check your state laws on how much equity in your home can be exempt if the judgment creditor tries to force a sale on your home.

Is there any way I can become judgment proof?

Yes, if you have no assets for the creditor to take, it will be a waste of their time trying to pursue you. If you are elderly, make less than $292.50 per week, are living on social security, being chased by the IRS, are behind on child support payments, plan on leaving the country for good, are living on disability, or have several judgments against you, then you are judgment proof. The following income is protected against creditors:

Income protected:

- Social Security and Social Security disability
- Veterans Benefits
- Retirement Pensions
- Welfare Benefits
- Unemployment Benefits
- Child Support
- Spousal Support

Assets protected:

- Personal property not to exceed $1,000
- Security deposit used to secure your apartment
- Tax refund derived from the earned income tax credit
- Tools of your trade, maximum protection 10,000 (check your state law)
- Homestead house or mobile home (check your state law)
- One vehicle (check your state law)

If you get a notice that the creditor is trying to seize your income or your personal assets, file your state exemption right away. Immediacy is important because the law only allows a certain amount of time for you to file your exemption.

Wage Garnishment

What is a wage garnishment?

A wage garnishment can be initiated after the creditor gets a judgment against you for the debt you owe. The creditor will contact a sheriff who will send the garnishment paperwork to your employer. This allows money to be taken from your paycheck until the judgment is satisfied.

How long can my check be garnished?

It depends on your state law. Some states allow the creditor to pull money once, and other states allow the creditor to garnish your wages until the debt is satisfied. Check your state law for further information on this matter.

What kinds of wages are exempt from garnishment?

- Welfare
- Unemployment
- Veteran benefits
- Social security
- Workers compensation
- Child support
- Pension

How much can be taken out of my check?

Again, check with your state on the amount that can be taken out. Most states allow up to 25% on regular debt. For child support or alimony, 50% can be taken out. If you support a second child or spouse, up to 60% could be taken from your paycheck. **See wage garnishment laws in the appendix.**

How do I stop a wage garnishment?

- You can stop this by filing a wage garnishment exemption with the court or with the levy officer within 10 days from the start of the garnishment. You want to claim that you cannot afford to have money taken because it will create a hardship for your family. In addition, it will prevent you from buying the basic needs like food. Only present this argument if you will indeed experience a hardship. If you file a claim for exemption and the creditor fails to challenge it within a certain amount of time allowed by the court, the judge may set the garnishment to the side.

- You, or a lawyer, may file a motion to set aside, suppress, or void a writ of garnishment due to a lack of jurisdiction or unlawful bases. You can challenge the writ by stating that you never owed the debt to begin with, or that the statute of limitation to collect it has expired. You can also argue for inaccuracy, or that an improper person is identified as the debtor.

- When settling, make sure you get a release to prevent the creditor from trying to collect the difference. Moreover, get a satisfaction of judgment letter. This document tells the court that the debt has been paid in full.

- If the debt is too big and your negotiations fail, you can file bankruptcy. After initiating a bankruptcy, you must let your employer, the creditor's attorney, and the levy officers know by sending them a copy of the voluntary petition. This will stop the wage garnishment. For more information on wage garnishment, check Title 111 of the Consumer Credit Practice Act. **See a sample satisfaction of judgment letter in the appendix section.**

Car Repossession

How can I stop the bank from taking my car?

When you default on your financial obligations, the lender will use the courts to take back property that is secured by a loan.

- If you can't afford the vehicle, try to sell it and pay the difference in your loan.

- You can also refinance it if possible.

- Ask your lender if you can add the delinquent amount to the end of the loan.

- Voluntarily surrender it to avoid the car from being repossessed. If you let the repo man take the car, two things will happen. There will be more fees involved because the bank had to hire a company to come out and pick up the car. And the word repossession will be placed on your credit report, which is more damaging than voluntary repossession.

How can I get my car back?

According to the law, you have a certain amount of time to reinstate the vehicle. Call the bank and ask them how much time you have to pay the back payments, late penalty and repossession fees. **Check nfa.org for your state repossession laws.**

What if I owe a balance on my car after the auction?

Once your repossessed car has been sold in the auction, you will receive the deficiency amount (the amount you owed from your original loan minus the auction sale price and fees) from the bank. You can try to settle the debt for 20 cents on the dollar. You can also set up a payment plan to settle the balance, and then subsequently challenge the item. If you don't posses the money to pay, it will go to a collector and possibly to court if it's a large amount. If this happens, follow the strategies used for collection agencies and judgments. **See nfa.org for car repossession laws in your state.**

What if I'm sued for the deficiency amount?

You can go to prepaidlegal.com and sign up for a membership to speak with a lawyer. Once you have found a lawyer, talk with him or her about the various arguments listed below. These defenses can be used to cancel the deficiency amount.

Arguments you can use:

- You have evidence that the mileage disclosure was false.
- The car sale was not commercially reasonable according to the law.
- The dealer failed to display the Federal Buyers Guide as required by Federal Law.
- Upon financing, you did not receive a completed sales agreement in a format required by the Federal law.

- Most state statutes list a category of deceptive trade practices (Check your state statute to see if the dealer or the creditor violated any of these practices).

- If your car was sold with a written warranty and was taken back to the dealer for repairs, you may have an argument if the dealer refused to fix it.

- Any breach in warranty is considerable.

- The creditor did not send you a written notice advising you that they would sell the car, and that you would have a certain amount of time to redeem (pay off) the vehicle before it was sold.

- Dealers are required by law to let you know that the car was either wrecked, rebuilt, salvaged, stolen, water-damaged or a buy back lemon. If they did not disclose this information, and it caused you some type of damage, you can use this as an argument.

- Some states require dealers to inspect the engine and drive train on cars purchased after October 1, 1997. The dealer must give the buyer a written disclosure of any defects. If your car breaks down after you leave the lot, then you can use this argument because the dealer did not disclose the problem with the car.

How do I get late car payments off of my credit report?

You want to make the lender prove that you were late for those days indicated on your credit report. Call the loan company and ask them to send you proof that you were behind on your bill. If they can't provide you with proof, contact the credit bureau by letter and advise them that the bank has not provided you with proof and that the late entry should to be deleted from your report.

Student Loans

I have defaulted on my student loan? What will happen?

You are considered in default once your payment is 270 days behind. Once this takes place, the lending institution can come after you with the power of the government. The entire balance of the loan will become due. You will not be eligible for a deferment or forbearance. There is no statute of limitation on collections. You can't discharge the loan in bankruptcy. You can't get further loans. The school may withhold your transcripts, and your tax refund will be intercepted. Your wages can be garnished. Your credit report will be damaged, collection fees will be added to your balance, liens can be placed on your personal and real property, and your bank accounts and other assets can be seized.

How do I get out of default status?

- Ask the lender for a payment plan based on your income.

- Try to get into the loan rehabilitation program. With this plan, you make 12 on time payments, and then a new lender will buy your loan providing you with a fresh payment plan and a lower monthly payment.

- Consolidate all of your defaulted loans. You will get a better interest rate and payment plan under a different lender.

- Settle your balance by seeking a compromise with the lender.

- File for bankruptcy after proving undue hardship. You must show that your present income is too low to pay the loan, and there are various steps you must take to prove your case.

- File a Chapter 13, and your interest, collection attempts, wage garnishments, and tax refund interception will stop while you are paying back your loan.

Can I defend myself against the student loan collectors?

If a private collection agency is used to collect the debt, and the agency violates the Fair Debt Collection Practices Act, you can sue them and use the money to pay off your debt. If you are sued, you can argue that you were eligible for a loan cancellation according to the student loan policies, but did not get it.

Is there anyway I can cancel the student loan?

The loan can be canceled if you are disabled and can't work, in the military, teaching in a third world country, performing community service, working as a health care professional in needy populations, or working in law enforcement. Check with your student loan provider for various options. You can also have your loan interest rates lowered if you consolidate your loans or set up an automatic debit for your payment. For more information on student loans, **contact the Federal Student Aid Information Center at 1-800-433-3243 or visit them at www.nslds.ed.gov or the Direct Loan Servicing Center at 1-800-848-0979.**

Can I remove a defaulted student loan from my report?

If the student loan commission reported the delinquent account, the only way to remove it is to pay off the loan in full. You can then dispute it with the creditor bureau. The credit bureau will have to verify the information with the student loan commission. Since the commission has to administer so many loans, it is very possible that the commission may not verify with the credit bureau that your loan was ever in default.

Are there any programs to help with my payments?

Talk with your lender and ask them about the following loan payback options:

- *Standard Repayment Plan:*
  This is your basic payment plan when you graduate. With this plan, you will have a higher payment, but you would save more in the long run because you would pay less interest than if you had the payments extended out.

- *Graduated Repayment Plan:*
  In this plan, your payment starts out low and increases overtime.

- *Extended Repayment Plan:*
  With this option, you stretch the payments out over 15 to 30 years. Your payments will be lower but you will pay more interest.

- *Income Contingent or Income Sensitive Repayment Plan:*
  In this program, your payment is based on your annual income, family size, and loan amount. This is a government-associated program, in which the remaining amount of the loan will be forgiven after making payments for up to 10 or 20 years.

- *Accelerated Payment:*
  If you start out with a good job, you can pay extra money toward your loan, therefore, reducing your interest and your payment time.

Medical Bills

How do I deal with medical bills?

When you get a medical bill, look it over for errors like repeat procedures. Contact the hospital, and ask them for an audit of the bill. If the debt is too overwhelming, try to negotiate it for 20 cents on the dollar or set up a payment plan. If the billing department won't work with you, they will most likely send your account to a collection agency. You can send the agency a cease and desist letter (instructing the collection agency to stop contacting you) and the account will go right back to the hospital. At this point, send the hospital a settlement letter to start negotiations.

If you feel as though the doctor has doubled billed you for a procedure or did not perform to standard and a collection agency is trying to collect on the bill, you can threaten a malpractice suit. This should force the collection agency to back down. You can also threaten to file a complaint with the State Licensing Board, Better Business Bureau, and Local Medical Society.

If you don't have the money to pay for the bill, ask the hospital or the medical center about the charity funds. Many charities donate funds to the hospital for people who can't afford to pay for the medical service. The billing department won't automatically tell you about this source of income, so you must ask them.

Back Taxes

If you get an audit notice from the IRS, have a certified CPA go over your notice. CPA experts are versed in tax returns that contain mistakes and need adjustments. Otherwise, letters from the IRS with words like "fraud" and "illegal" should be forward to a tax attorney.

How do I avoid a tax lien from hitting my credit report?

First make the IRS prove that you owe the debt. If they do provide you with proof, you must either pay the full amount or ask for a payment plan using IRS form 9465. In the payment plan, you can get up to 36 months to pay back the debt. This method can be used while you are applying for the Offer in Compromise. If your debt is very large, you can apply for an Offer in Compromise with the IRS. This program allows you to settle your bill and eliminate interest and fees. Look up OIC form 656 for more information. **For IRS forms go to IRS.gov.**

How do I get a negative paid tax lien debt off of my credit report?

Once you have paid the debt, ask the IRS to send you a Certificate of Release of the lien. This document states that you are released from the lien and no longer owe money. Most paid tax liens or IRS debts can be challenged with the basic dispute method. Old debts are removed more easily because they are moved to the archived files after two years, and the government does not have the time or resources to respond to every dispute on a paid bill.

What happens if I don't pay my back taxes?

If your back taxes are not paid, the IRS can stop you from getting a student loan. They can also take your tax return, place a federal tax lien on your home and force a sale. Your personal property can be seized along with your bank accounts, your IRA accounts, work income, life insurance policy with cash value and pension plans. Your alimony payments, license, franchise rights, royalties, and inheritance proceeds can be taken. As you can see, you can't get away from the government.

Is there anyway I can stop them?

The IRS has three years from the date you file to let you know that you owe back taxes. If they inform you after the statute has expired. You could hire an attorney and sue in court using the statute as an argument. If you did not file your taxes, there is no statute for your attempt to evade taxes. Furthermore, the IRS has 10 years from the date of assessment to collect taxes owed. If you believe that the money owed is not correct, you can have an attorney file an action in the U.S. Tax court challenging the notice. This matter can be in court for a long time, therefore, allowing you to be in a better position to settle with the IRS.

Bankruptcies

Can a bankruptcy be removed from my credit report?

When someone's debts exceed their annual income, they turn to the federal law where they surrender their assets to a third party trustee who sells them to pay off outstanding debts. Any other debts left accept for child support, student loans, back taxes, and alimony is discharged. Bankruptcies can be removed though they take time, so wait at least two years before you start disputing. The reason for this is that files go dead, and they are moved to storage.

You'll first want to dispute the individual items listed inside of the bankruptcy using the normal dispute method. You should then dispute items like incorrect names, dates, the amount of discharge, and the case number. Once you get rid of the accounts listed inside of the bankruptcies, it will be easier for you to delete the bankruptcy's listing. The reason for this is the bankruptcy's records are stored in the archives, which makes it harder for the credit bureau to investigate and respond back to you in 30 days.

A discharged bankruptcy debt is still showing that I owe.

If the debt was discharged, it must show zero on your credit report. The account should also say that it was included in the bankruptcy. Your listing should appear as Chapter 13 or 7. Some of the agencies still trying to collect may report the debt as open. These agencies are violating the Fair Debt Collection Practices Act (a law that regulates collection agencies) and the bankruptcy code. Write to the credit bureaus and the collection agencies letting them know that you may hire an attorney and file a lawsuit for violation of the bankruptcy code.

Foreclosure

What is foreclosure?

When an owner of a home defaults on their loan, their rights to own that property are terminated. This will result in a force sale of the home in a public auction.

What are some steps I can take to prevent a foreclosure?

- Talk with the HUD counseling agency for more options.
- Ask the bank to suspend your payments for a couple of months until you get back on your feet.
- Argue that you did not understand loan agreement when you first bought the house.
- Try a loan modification. With this option, the lender modifies several terms of your loan, like the payment, interest and sometimes the principal.

- See if the bank will go for a Short Sale. This is when you are selling the property at the current market value, and the price is lower than your original loan.

- Ask the bank if they will take a deed in lieu of foreclosure. Here, you voluntarily turn over the title to the lender to avoid foreclosure and damage to your credit report.

- Try refinancing before letting your home foreclose. With this option, the lender will construct a new loan for you with a better interest rate and payment plan. This method is impossible if you are underwater.

- Research the procedures on how foreclosure notices should be sent out, and if any of the steps were violated contact an attorney for a possible lawsuit. By doing this, it will slow down the foreclosure proceedings.

- File Chapter 7 bankruptcy as a last resort because it stops all foreclosure activity. You should be aware that the lender might ask the judge for a lift of stay, which would allow the foreclosure to proceed.

- File a Chapter 13 to stop the foreclosure. By doing this you are telling the bank that you need time to work out your financial situation. From there, you will be put on a payment plan to start paying back all of your creditors including the lender.

Keep looking into other options.

Ask for a repayment plan. Payments are increased to make up for the past due payments. You can make up these payments over a short or a long period of time. For example, if you are three months behind with a monthly payment of $400 a month, you can stretch out the $1200 over 12 months where you would pay a extra $100 a month on top of your regular payment.

Look into the Obama Plan-Harp-Home Affordable Modification Program. This plan is geared toward homeowners who are underwater in their loan. Harp allows you to rewrite your mortgage for a better interest rate and to convert from an adjustable rate to a fixed rate. **For more information, go to www.hmpadmin.com**

Look into the Obama Plan and Loan modification. In this plan, you are on a three-month trial period. During this time, you must make all your payments on time. Concluding the trial period, if there were no changes in your financial situation. The loan will continue to be modified at a reduced payment. Moreover, during the trial period, any foreclosure will be suspended. Be advised that if you have good credit when entering the trial period, it could hurt your credit. The reason it could damage your credit is the lender is reporting a modification of the loan and not the original loan.

What is mediation?

It is a process where the homeowner and the lender meet in person to exchange information and discuss ways to avoid foreclosure. A mediator facilitates this meeting.

Can mediation stop foreclosure?

Mediation can slow the foreclosure down, but it won't stop it, unless you and the bank come to an agreement during mediation.

Do all states offer the mediation program?

No, some states offer the mediation program while others do not. Check with your lender or consult with a real estate attorney on this matter.

How does the process work?

After you default on your loan, 90 days to 120 later the bank will send you a Default and Election to Sell Notice along with a mediation form. You must note that every state is different with this procedure. If you choose mediation, you have 30 days to return the mediation form. After you return the document, a mediation will be scheduled for you and the bank. During the mediation, you try to work out various options with the bank on how to avoid foreclosure such as the options listed above and in the bullet point section. If no agreement is made, the bank will continue with foreclosing on your home.

After foreclosure, when can the lender sue for the deficiency amount?

Every state is different, but they can usually sue six months after the foreclosure date, so check your state laws for the correct amount of time.

What about the deficiency on the second mortgage?

If you have a second mortgage on your home and your first mortgage forecloses, in some states the lender has six years to come after you for the deficiency amount on the second mortgage.

Do I have to pay the deficiency amount?

Check with your state to see whether lenders are allowed to collect the deficiency amounts. In some states, the deficiency judgment is automatically entered against you, and in other states the lender must sue you. Talk with an attorney for your options, and see whether you qualify for the Mortgage Debt Forgiveness Program. In this program, the lender forgives the loan debt, and you will receive an IRS 1099 at the end of the year. The 1099 displays the amount of money the bank forgave, and it will be counted as income according to the IRS. You will be responsible for paying taxes on the deficiency amount listed in the 1099. Lastly, you may consider filing for bankruptcy if the back debt is so high that it's causing you a hardship.

Can I remove a foreclosure deficiency from my report?

Wait about two years and allow the foreclosure files to be moved to the storage unit. At this time, you can begin your basic dispute method. Remember, when you dispute files that are old, the bank sometime choose not to verify the debt due to time constraints. If you are sued for the deficiency amount, you will need to hire an attorney to help you settle this matter. You can argue that you surrendered the home. You paid off the loan, or you entered into a Deed In-Lieu of Foreclosure. You can also settle the balance for 30 cents on the dollar. With large deficiencies over 75,000, you should probably start talking to a bankruptcy lawyer.

Key points to remember

- Use a good will letter for late payments
- Dispute the information inside of a charge off listing
- Try to get the judgment vacated
- Dispute the accounts inside of the bankruptcy listing
- Review your state laws on car repossession
- Try to settle your medical bill or complain to the medical board and other agencies
- Set up a payment agreement and look into the Offer in Compromised with the IRS back taxes

- Seek out payment options you may have through the student loan organization

- Explore different options to avoid foreclosure

Chapter 5:

How to Repair My Credit With Debt Settlement Techniques

Shirley's Story

One day, while having coffee with a friend at Starbucks, a woman sitting nearby us overheard our conversation on debt settlement and asked if she could interrupt. Her name was Shirley, and she said that she was intrigued by our mention of negotiating debt for mere "pennies on the dollar." I said, "Yes! It seems unlikely, but this is a common debt settlement technique." She went on to describe her own financial trouble in detail, including harassing calls from several collection agencies. She asked if I could help her, and I was more than happy to.

"Sure I can assist you," I said, "but you have to have cash when you are trying to settle with collectors and creditors." The next day, I drafted a debt settlement letter for Shirley and emailed it to her. Three weeks later, she called me, happy and grateful, and said, "Mark with that one letter I sent, it allowed me to settle three of my debts for 30 cents on the dollar. Just like you said!"

The moral of the story is education is power. If Shirley had not taken action by having the courage to ask about debt settlement, the courage to send out the letters, or the courage to finally confront her debt, her credit would still be damaged today.

TAKE ACTION NOW!

Settling debts for pennies on the dollar takes cash, patience, and knowledge. This technique is one of the most powerful ways to get creditors and collection agencies to stop calling you and to remove negative items from your credit report. You have something creditors want, and that is money. But in order to interact with collectors, you must also possess the right communication skills to win. Once you master the techniques on debt settlement, you will be able to take your credit worthiness to a whole different level.

Which accounts should I settle first?

Before contacting the creditor, review your credit report to determine which accounts should be negotiated. Look for charge off accounts, debts that have been sold to a third party collection agency and old judgments.

Why is the federal statute of limitation so important?

The statute of limitations is critical because you may be paying for an old debt that has passed a deadline and is getting ready to fall off your credit report. Take a look at the date the account went delinquent and then look at the federal statute located in the appendix. If the statute has expired, it's time for the negative item to come off of your credit report. Now, view your outdated accounts again focusing on the date of last activity. Review your state statute located in the appendix to see if your debt has expired. If so, the creditor can't collect by way of suing you for a judgment, but they can still continue their collection efforts.

Ok, now I want the creditor to prove that it's my debt.

Right before you settle, write the creditor a letter asking them to provide you with written proof that you owe the debt. Ask them to send you the original application bearing your signature. Federal law requires creditors to provide proof upon request by the consumer. Give the creditor 16 days to respond to your request. If they don't write back, send the creditor bureau a letter asking for a deletion because the creditor can't prove that you owe the debt. Write the attorney general's office in the creditor's state, and let the attorney general know that the creditor is reporting negative information on your credit report even though they can't prove that you owe the debt.

What debts can be settled?

The easiest debts to settle are unsecured debts like medical bills, credit cards, retail store cards, personal loans, old collection accounts, outdated judgments, and charge offs. The reason why you can negotiate these debts is because the lenders have no collateral against them if you decided to default. Secured debts like your home and car are almost impossible to settle since the lender has a lien on the property, but you can settle the deficiency amount if the car is taken or the house goes into foreclosure.

Why would they settle?

- Lenders feel that once you get 90 to 120 days behind, you may not pay your debt.

- If you file bankruptcy, the banks would have to take a loss.

- They would rather settle then sell the debt to a collector for 10 cents on the dollar.

- They also know that you have no assets, so they can't sue, and if they do go to court, it will cost more than the value of the debt.

They won't settle, why?

- Most banks and lenders will negotiate, but some won't if they believe that you have enough assets to pursue a judgment.
- You are current on other financial obligations.
- The debt has not been charged off yet.
- Your payments are current.
- You offered a 30% settlement on a payment plan.

What day is the best time to settle?

For creditors, the perfect time to settle your debt is once your debt gets closer to the charge off date. Once you have fallen behind on your payments for 180 days or 6 months, they will be more likely to negotiate a better deal because they feel that they are going to take a loss. With collection agencies, the end of the month is the best time since the agents have quotas to make and commissions to claim.

How late should I be before settling?

The older the debt is the better the negotiations. Some banks start accepting settlements at three months behind, but most will start negotiations after or right before 180 days. If you negotiate after this date, you may have to deal with a collection agency.

How do I avoid collections?

To stop the bank from sending your account to collections, you must start your negotiations at 150 days; before the charge off date. This will avoid the debt from being charged off and going to collections, and you will be able to strike a better deal with the original creditor.

What happens when the account is charged off?

The creditor will take a tax write off for the bad debt, and the lender can either sell or assign your debt to a collection agency or to the pre-legal department for a possible lawsuit.

Can I record the conversation with the creditor?

Yes, and no; it depends on your state laws. If your state is a one party state, then you do not need the creditor's permission to record the conversation because you need only one person's authorization, and that is yours. In a two party state, you do need the creditor's permission to record the conversation. **See state laws on recording conversations over the phone in the appendix.**

Should I document my contact with the creditor?

Yes, always document and keep correspondences between yourself, the creditor, and the collection agency. Furthermore, keep all letters and envelopes from the creditor as the envelopes show the dates they were sent. Documentation is needed in case you have to go to court and prove to the judge that you tried to settle the debt.

How many creditors or collection agencies should I deal with at one time?

Settle with each creditor or collection agency one at a time. For example, find out how much you owe on the first debt, then call them up or send a settlement letter. Once you have negotiated a deal, start with the second creditor. If you call up multiple creditors at one time, you may run out of money to settle your debts.

Should I write or call?

When dealing with the original creditor, you should call them because they are not as cold as the collection agencies. Moreover, send all settlement letters via certified mail with return receipt to collection agencies as they have a habit of not honoring their agreements.

What should I say?

Contact the creditor by phone and ask them for the customer service department. Don't admit that the debt is yours, or you can restart the state statute of limitation. Politely provide them with your account number and inquire whether their company offers settlements. Keep your conversation short and straight to the point.

How do I negotiate? What are some key phrases I can use?

Don't appear to look desperate for a settlement because the creditor may use it against you. For example, don't say, "I need to clear this debt, so that I can buy a house or a car." Here are a few examples of opening negotiation tactics you might want to consider:

- I don't have the amount you are looking for, but I can settle for this amount today.

- I'm actually considering filing for bankruptcy since I don't have the amount you are asking for. Is there something we can work out?

- My financial situation is getting worse, but if I can come up with a lump sum would you settle for this amount by tomorrow?

How much should I offer?

Before making a settlement, set the amount you will start with and the highest percentage you will settle for, for example, you can start at 20%, but your max will be 35%. Banks start high like 80%, and the lowest they will go is 30%. Always try to get the lender to meet you in the middle as this can be done during the counter offer stage. You can start with 20 cents on the dollar and move up to your max negotiation price. Use dollar amounts when speaking rather than simply saying "20 cents on the dollar." The dollar amount is a concrete term that can be more easily grasped and referenced back to. If you can't make the lump sum, negotiate a partial payment now and three payments over the next three months.

What if the creditors won't settle?

- You can wait a week and call them back asking to speak with the supervisor and offer the same settlement.

- Repeat the process every week moving up the management chain until you reach the president.

- Send a letter stating that you need a response right away because the other creditors have accepted your agreement, and you will have to start the plan without them.

- Wait until the creditor sends you another balance due letter. You can counter with a settlement letter.

- Retain a bankruptcy lawyer and have him send the creditor a letter stating you are considering bankruptcy.

- Hang up and call again to get another representative.

- You could pay the original balance without the fees. If the original balance is taken care of, the creditor or the collection agency can't report only the interest and fees to the credit bureau.

How do I negotiate my credit rating?

For exchange of your payment, ask the creditor to delete the negative item on your report. If you can't get a deletion, go for a paid as agreed, current account or unrated status. Avoid negative listings like account closed, paid, paid charge off, settled or repossession. In addition, you want paid in full with no further collection on this account indicated in your agreement. If the creditor does not agree with any of your requests, don't pay them.

What should I include in the agreement?

Go to prepaidlegal.com and sign up for a $17 membership. Once you have selected a lawyer, have him or her review your agreement. Make sure your terms are in the agreement before sending any money. You can draw up the settlement or wait for the creditor to send it to you. Send your agreement out and wait for the creditor or collection agency to sign it before sending it back. Ask the creditor to send the settlement by fax followed by a letter.

What about paying them?

Once the creditor signs the agreement, you can send the payment with a copy of the settlement agreement by a wire transfer, western union, quick collect, overnight mail or Fed Ex. Please do not use a check because the creditor will obtain your checking information and start taking out payments. Instead, use a cashier's check, money order, or a prepaid credit card with the exact amount. Make sure you keep and store your receipts in a safe place.

What if I don't keep my agreement? What can happen?

If you don't meet your obligation, the creditor will reinstate your original terms and add late fees and over the limit fees. In addition, your interest rates will go up and you can possibly be sued.

What if they try to collect the difference in my settlement?

In some states, these actions are illegal, and you will have to write the creditor and let them know that. Other states allow collectors to come after you for the difference. If this is the case, you will find that the creditor has written or stamped the words "under protest" or "without prejudice" on your check. **See appendix for states.**

How is the IRS involved in the debt settlement?

When a creditor settles a debt for less than what's owed, they have forgiven the difference on what you owed. The creditor must report any monies forgiven over $600 to the IRS for tax purposes. The creditor will also send you a 1099-c indicating the amount you saved in the settlement. Because you got a deal, the IRS considers the money as a gain to you and therefore, income. By law, you are required to pay taxes on this gain.

Should I check my credit report after the settlement?

Yes, get a current copy of your credit report to see whether the creditor has honored their agreements. If there is no change, contact the creditor and remind them of their obligation.

What if I'm dealing with a collection agency?

All communication and settlements must take place by mail with certified return receipts. If you are contacted by a collection agency, ask for their name, address, and agency they are calling from. You will need this information to start writing letters. When negotiating, use the techniques mentioned in this chapter. Before you start negotiation, use the debt validation strategy to make sure the debts are yours. **See validation techniques in chapter six.**

What negotiating powers do the creditors give the collection agencies?

If the account is assigned, creditors must give the collection agency authorization to negotiate your debt starting from 15% to 50%.

The collection agency said that they couldn't change the credit status.

Speak with a supervisor or someone in authority to make the change. You can also tell the collector to get a letter of agreement from the creditor about the status change and tell them that you are willing to pay them. You can also advise the collection agency that by making a settlement, you are entering into a new agreement, which will change the status of your account on your credit report, and therefore, they can allow the negative items to be deleted.

How can I stop them from suing me?

Send the collection agency the amount you tried to agree on, and that should stop them from filing a lawsuit because they have most of the money you owed.

What if I receive a notice that they are suing me?

You have a certain amount of time to respond to this lawsuit notice, so send in your answer along with a settlement agreement to the creditor's attorney. If that does not work, and you feel that the creditor or collection agency has violated the FCRA or FDCPA, you can initiate a counter claim.

Be aware that the creditor or collection agency will try to scare you into settlement. They may threaten you with any of the following tactics:

- Warning you that your debt will be placed into charge off status

- Asking you to fill out an asset questionnaire

- Warning you that your account is in legal, but you can stop it if you pay now

- Placing you on hold and running your offer by a supervisor

- Giving you 48 hours to decide on the settlement offer

- Warning you that they are in the process of suing you

- They use fear and intimidation to get you to settle, but ignore their threats and keep negotiating.

Key points to remember

- Review the state statute of limitation on the debt

- Have the creditor prove that it's your debt first

- Always try settling right before 180 days
- Start your negotiations out at 20 cents on the dollar
- Negotiate for a complete deletion of the negative item
- Make sure all of your terms are in the agreement
- Send only a cashier check or money order, or wire transfer
- Don't forget once you settle, you may have to pay taxes

Chapter 6:

Can I Stop the Collection Agencies in Their Tracks?

Mark's Story

One morning, while having my coffee and checking the mail, I noticed a letter from an attorney's office located in New York. It was unusual for me to receive a letter from a law firm in another state, so I opened the letter only to find a larger surprise: it was a debt collection letter. The letter stated that I owed money and that if I did not pay I would be sued. Well, I knew very well that I did not owe this debt, so I immediately went online to the state web site that issues licenses to collection agencies.

I put the attorney's law firm name into the search bar and it came back "not found." This suggested that the out of state attorney was violating the law by trying to collect a debt despite having no license to do so. My suspicions were confirmed when I sent a validation letter to the attorney asking him to send me a copy of his license and bond authorizing him to collect in my state, a copy of the original contract with my signature, and the contract allowing him to collect the debt for the creditor.

I sent the letter certified mail with a return receipt, but I never heard from the attorney again. This was three years ago. The moral of the story is education is power. If I had not known which steps to take, I might have been frightened into paying the debt just to avoid being sued.

TAKE ACTION NOW!

Collection agencies are at the bottom of the barrel when it comes down to business. The only thing they care about is cold, hard cash. They don't care if you've just lost your job, your spouse, or your health. Their job is to bleed you of money, whichever way they can. However, you can stop them in their tracks by applying your newfound knowledge and the law. There are several tactics you can use in standing up to a collection agency, including saying the right words, sending a detailed letter, or quoting the law.

What is a collection agency?

Collection agencies are third party companies that use aggressive tactics to collect outstanding debts from consumers. Old debts are either assigned or sold to the collector by a creditor. If the debt is assigned, once the collector obtains the money, a percentage of it is kept by the agency, and the remaining goes to the creditor. If the collector buys debts for 10 cents on the dollar, they own it, and they will want 100% from you.

Why was my account turned over to a collection agency?

- The bank could not locate you or contact you
- Your debt is over 120 days late
- You moved out of state and they still can't reach you

Those are the primary reasons why a lender or a credit card company would assign or sell your debt to a collection agency.

What law regulates collection agencies?

The Fair Debt Collection Practices Act regulates the collection agencies and prohibits them from doing the following:

- They can only contact a third party to secure your location, but they cannot disclose the matter of the call.

- After the collection agency knows that you have legal representation, they must communicate only with your attorney, unless the attorney fails to respond within a reasonable time.

- They cannot call you before 8am or after 9pm.

- If your employment prohibits personal phone calls, they cannot call your job.

- The collector cannot discuss your debt with any third party unless it's your attorney, a credit bureau, the creditor, or the creditor's attorney.

- If you notify the collector in writing that you want them to stop calling and sending you letters, they must stop. They can still send you one last letter advising you what actions they will take next.

- They cannot harass, oppress, abuse, threaten use of violence, use obscene or profane language, cause your telephone to ring repeatedly with the intent to be annoying, or make calls to your house without disclosing their identity.

They may not use any false, deceptive, or misleading representation while trying to collect any debt. They can't appear to be affiliated with any government or law enforcement agency, representation that they are attorneys, threaten to garnish your wages, or say that they can have you arrested and imprisoned. Furthermore, they cannot threaten to take action that cannot be legally taken. In addition, they may not use unfair or unconscionable means to collect or attempt to collect any debt. They cannot collect interest, fees, or charges (unless authorized by a signed agreement with you) or threaten to deposit a postdated check issued by you.

They must obtain verification of the debt or a copy of the judgment and mail it out to you upon request within 30 days. If you dispute the debt within the 30 days of receiving a notice from the collector, they must cease collection of the debt until they obtain verification of the debt.

If you have multiple debts with one collection agency, they must apply the payment to the debt you advised them to pay.

What about creditor's in-house collectors?

The in-house collection agencies are not subject to the Fair Debt Credit Practicing Act, so if you send them a Cease and desist letter it has no weight. The Federal Trade Commission Act prohibits an unfair or deceptive trade practices. If you feel that the creditor's collection agency violated the FTC Act, you can seek sanctions. Example of a violation, the collector calling your job when you can't have personal phone calls. You can also file a complaint with your local attorney general's office and that should stop the in-house collectors. Now, some states subject the in-house collectors to the FDCPA so check with your state laws.

I received a call and a letter from the collection agency. What do I do?

First, you want the collection agency to prove that it's your debt. Send them a debt validation letter right away via certified mail and with a return receipt. Don't wait, because you may miss the 30-day deadline, which gives the collector the right to report this debt to the credit bureau if you do not dispute it. **See sample letter in the appendix.**

In your validation letter, let them know not to send you a computer printout itemizing your outstanding debt, as this is not sufficient proof according to the FTC. Instead, ask the collector to provide you with a copy of the following:

- Their bond and license to collect in your state
- A copy of the agreement authorizing them to collect debt on behalf of the creditor
- An accounting statement on how they reached the amount you supposedly owe
- A copy of the contract you signed with the creditor bearing your signature
- The name and address of the creditor

If within 30 days, the collection agency sends you the proof that you requested, and the debt is really yours, try to settle the outstanding amount for pennies on the dollar using the strategies outlined in the negotiation section. Make sure you do this before the collection agency reports the negative item to the credit bureau 30 days from the date you received the letter.

What if they did not respond to my validation letter?

Pull your credit report to see whether the collection agency has reported the outstanding debt. If the bill is there, send the collector a certified letter with a return receipt stating that they have violated the FDCPA by collecting and reporting negative information on to your credit report without validating it.

In your letter, demand that they delete the information immediately, and include copies of the first certified return receipt mailing and your letter you sent. Give them 16 days to respond to your demand. In the meantime, write a letter to the credit bureau asking them to delete the damaging item because the collection agency was not able to verify the debt.

During this time, if the collection agency has not responded or has not deleted the incorrect item, file a complaint with the FTC and your local attorney general's office. Wait for the credit bureau to respond to you. If they respond saying that the negative item was verified by the collection agency, then it may be time to take legal action. With enough grounds, you can sue them for Defamation and violation of the FDCPA.

They responded to my validation letter with a summons?

Write back to them stating that they cannot sue you if they have not validated the debt. If the debt goes to court, argue that the collection agency did not validate the debt according to the law.

I don't have the money to pay, what can I do?

Send the debt validation letter. If it comes back validated, set up a payment plan right away to avoid the debt from damaging your credit report using the negotiation strategies in chapter five.

How did the collector find me?

They use an investigative technique called skip tracing. The agency use computer databases that give them access to your credit report, current and past addresses, voter registration card, DMV records, and other sources with your information on it.

The debt they said that I owe is not mine?

Send the creditor and the collection agency a validation letter within 30 days of receiving their notice. At the same time, pull a copy of your credit report to see whether the debt has been reported. If the negative item has not been reported, wait for your validation letter, which should prove that you do not owe the debt.

If the item is being reported on your credit report, send a second letter to the credit bureau and collection agency disputing it and stating that they are in violation of the FCPA and the FDCPA. State that they must delete the item now, or you will file a lawsuit. If you do hear back from the credit bureau and collector stating that the debt is yours, then file a complaint with the FTC and the attorney general's office. In addition, talk with an attorney about seeking damages and an injunctive relief in small claims court.

How do I stop them from harassing me?

Send them a cease and desist letter by certified mail with return receipt, which directs the collector to stop all contact with you. At this point, the collection agency will give the account back to the creditor or turn it over to an attorney. Once the original creditor receives the account, it will be sold to another collection agency, turned over to an attorney for a suit, or charged off.

What if they violate the law?

Send the creditor a letter stating that their collection agency is harassing you and violating the law. Most creditors want to keep you as a customer, so they may intervene and tell the collector to back off. During that time, start building your case against the collector by keeping a journal. Things you should keep track of include times and dates, names of persons you talked to, what they said that may constitute a violation of the law, letters sent to and from the collector, and vocal recordings of the conversation (if your state allows it). Finally, you may even want to have a third party listen in on your conversation and have them take notes. Make sure they are willing to act as witnesses in court for you, should the need arise. **See laws on recording conversation in the appendix.**

What should I say over the phone?

When the collector calls you, ask for their name, address, where they are calling from, call back number and the nature of the call. Never tell them where you work, if they ask. If they say, "Is this Mark I'm speaking with," be cooperative and say "Yes, how can I help you?" However, make sure that you never admit that you own the debt. Before they even start questioning you about the debt, ask them to send all information about the debt by mail, and then hang up.

What if it's a collection attorney that is calling me?

It's no difference, if the attorney collects two debts a year, then he has to adhere to the laws of the FDCPA. Don't let attorneys scare you. Most credit card companies employ lawyers to send out standard letters hoping that they will collect based off of the letters. If you get a demand letter from an out-of-state attorney asking for money, ask him to validate the debt and watch him go away. I know this from firsthand experience, and as you know, I never heard from him again. The validation letter works.

What are some of the collection agency phone tactics?

- They will use various tactics to try to get you to pay your debt.

- Once they get a judgment against you, they will keep calling you to try to get personal information to assist with their enforcement.

- They will threaten to criminally prosecute you for writing bad checks.

- A collector may threaten to take your home if the debt is not paid.

- They will also assemble information on you looking for a weakness.

- They will say that you have to deal with them and not the creditor.

How can I respond to them?

- You can respond by sending them a cease and desist letter.

- Ask them whether you can tape the call, which will force them to be courteous.

- Let them know that you will be contacting the original creditor about their abusive tactics.

- Let them know that you will consider legal action if they keep violating the law.

- Let them know that you know your rights, and if they violate them you will sue.

- If they are trying to collect for a professional, like a doctor or a CPA, threaten to file a complaint against the professional.

- Let them know you will complain to the FTC, attorney general's office, state licensing boards, and their collection organizations.

- If the state statute of limitation has expired and the collector tries to collect, let them know that they are in violation of the FDCPA.

Can they come after me if I move to another state?

No, the creditor cannot assign your debt to a collector in the new state you live in. They must try to collect only in the state that the debt was created in, unless you are sued and they get a judgment. If this happens, they can transfer the judgment to you in your new state.

Should I sign for certified mail?

No, because it gives the collection agency proof that you received their demand letter, and they can use it against you in court.

Should I send them a postdated check?

No, never send a post dated check because they will simply break the law and cash it before the cash date. This will put your checking account into the negative if you don't have the money to cover the check. Don't give out your account number when setting up a payment arrangement because they will debit what they want until the debt is satisfied. Just send them a money order from the post office or a cashier's check from a bank that you do not belong to.

Why do I care if the debt is assigned or bought?

With assigned accounts, the collection agency does not own the debt, and therefore you don't owe them any money unless you have a clause in your original contract stating that you are responsible for paying back the money to your creditor or whom they assign.

Why did the collection agency place little debts on my credit report?

They placed the small outstanding debts on your credit reports hoping that once you need a credit card, you would call them up and pay the bill.

What if they try to sue me over an expired debt?

Go to court and argue that the state statute of limitation of the debt has expired, and then file a counter claim claiming violation of the FDCPA for trying to collect on an outdated account. **See the state statute in the appendix.**

Key points to remember

- Always get the collection agency to validate the debt.
- Settle your debt only if they will delete the negative item.
- Study the Fair Debt Collection Practices Act.
- Collectors can track you down using skip tracing software.

- Send them a cease and desist letter to stop harassment.

Chapter 7:

How Can I Protect My Good Credit During a Divorce?

Tom's Story

A while ago, my friend Tom was going through a bad divorce. They had all of their financial accounts in both of their names, and with nowhere to turn for financial advice, Tom came to me for help. He wanted to know how could he remove his spouse's name from their joint accounts so that he could start a new financial life. I explained to Tom that his divorce decree did not break his obligations with the creditor because he and his spouse had both signed on the dotted line for their debts.

I advised him to cancel his joint accounts and open new ones solely in his name. I also advised him that taking these steps would prevent his credit from being destroyed in the event that his spouse refused to pay her portion of the bills according to the divorce decree. The moral of the story is that education is power. By taking offensive steps to protect his good credit, Tom safeguarded his solid credit history. Knowing the law made all the difference.

TAKE ACTION NOW!

Your credit is one of your greatest income builders, so protect it before, while, and after you are married. Often, couples act under the common misconception that once you are married, all credit accounts should be merged. This is far from the truth, or from necessity. When couples apply for joint accounts, financial negligence of one spouse causes the other to suffer. And though love may be for better or worse, your finances don't have to be. Educating yourself on how to handle finances while married is a key factor to a strong marriage and credit history.

Should I talk to my future wife or husband about their personal finances before we get married?

Yes. During the courting state and before you get married, you and your spouse should sit down and discuss the various aspects of your financial life. As you may know, money fights are one of the number one reasons that couples divorce. So before getting married, you should openly discuss the following topics with your fiancé:

- Comparing credit reports and scores
- Discuss financial goals
- Talk about budgeting
- Converse about spending patterns
- Discuss past due and outstanding debts
- Decide who will manage the bills
- Decide whether there will be joint or separate accounts
- Discuss how you and your spouse think about money

What if my spouse's credit is bad?

This will only be a problem when you are applying for joint accounts. Because your partner's score is bad, it could cause your loan to be denied, or you could pay higher interest rates. On the flip side, you can help your spouse rebuild credit by cosigning or by applying the methods explained in chapter eight on building your credit from ground up.

Will the credit card company add my spouses maiden name to her current credit card account?

Yes. She can have her new name reflect on her credit report and her credit card. She must let her credit card company know, and they will update the credit bureau and her account. When she pulls her credit report, her new name will still be there but her maiden name will be listed under the alias section.

How should we handle our finances while married?

Marriages are changing in this new era because people are used to their independence when it comes to money and credit. In order for a marriage to be successful when it comes to money, couples need to maintain their independence. Here is a list of key points that most couples should consider.

- Open separate checking and credit card accounts.
- Open one joint checking account for major bills.
- Open only one joint account for the purchase of a home.

- Your spouse should let your current creditor know that you want to keep your individual credit cards in your original name.

- Build a budget together.

- Start a retirement plan.

- Take out life insurance on each other.

- Monitor all joint accounts by using a monitor service or checking every 4 months.

- Create an emergency fund of at least three to six months of expenses.

What if I have a divorce decree?

Before you go to court, try to decide who is going to pay what. If your spouse is going to live in the home, then he or she should pay. This applies to your car as well. After the court case, send a copy of the divorce decree to all lenders. If your spouse violates the divorce decree, talk with a divorce attorney about your options. Even if you have a divorce decree stating one spouse should be required to pay certain bills, you are still responsible for paying that bill back to the bank because you and your spouse's names are both on the original contract.

What should we do about bills during the divorce?

Before you get divorced, make sure that you do the following:

Pull your credit report

Check your credit reports for joint accounts and authorized user accounts. Furthermore, check to make sure that your spouses information is not merged with yours. If there is an authorized user and a merged account, dispute it with the credit bureau asking them to separate the accounts and remove your spouses name from your credit report. Three months after the divorce is final, check your report again to make sure your spouse is not opening new accounts in your name. If so, dispute the items as identity theft and put a fraud alert and a credit freeze on your credit report.

Credit cards

Call the credit card companies and let them know that you want to pay off the balance of the cards and close the accounts due to circumstantial events. If your spouse is an authorized user, have him or her removed. You can then open new accounts in your name.

If your spouse is giving you a problem as to closing the accounts, have the credit card company freeze the accounts. Follow up with a letter to the lender reiterating that you want to close the account. Then order your credit report 30 days later to make sure your accounts have been closed. Once the divorce is over, send the creditors a copy of the decree, just in case there is a problem in the future.

Checking and Saving

You should split what's left in your joint account with your spouse, then close that account and open a new one in your name only.

House

If you have no kids, then you and your spouse can sell the house and split the proceeds. If your spouse decides to keep the house with the kids, then try to have the house refinanced with just his or her name on it. Do not sign a quitclaim deed or let your name be removed from the title because you will lose ownership and still be responsible for paying the loan. Make sure you have the mortgage payment sent to you to keep track of the payments.

Car

Try to sell it first and then split the proceeds. If the spouse wants the vehicle, try to have it refinanced in his or her name. If that is unsuccessful, keep your name on the title and make sure your spouse is paying the bill by having the statement come to your house.

What if my spouse files for bankruptcy?

Your spouse can file bankruptcy on his or her portion of the debt, and leave you hanging with the entire amount. To counter his or her actions talk with your bankruptcy lawyer about the Bankruptcy Reform Act of 1994. This law has made it hard for a spouse to eliminate debt owed under a property settlement agreement. If you feel that your spouse can pay their part, have your bankruptcy lawyer file an exception to the bankruptcy proceedings.

What is the Innocent Spouse Rule?

This happens when a spouse signs the tax returns not knowing what it contains, then they get divorced. The spouse can be held liable for any back taxes that are generated from that tax return. The innocent spouse relief law was enacted to fight this and to assist the spouse that had no idea of what was in the tax return. **For more information, see IRS publication 971 or go to www.irs.gov.**

What if I live in a community state?

If you live in a community state, you and your spouse automatically become joint owners when a credit card is open. Here is a list of those states.

- Arizona
- California
- Idaho
- Louisiana
- Nevada
- New Mexico
- Texas
- Washington
- Wisconsin
- Alaska

What if my spouse passed away?

If your state is not a community state, the creditor will want a copy of the death certificate along with monetary funds from your spouse's estate to pay the bad debt. Make sure you send a copy of the death certificate to the credit bureau to avoid your spouse's identity from being stolen. Most of the time, the Social Security Administration will notify the credit bureau of your spouse's death, and they will flag his or her account.

Key points to remember

- Talk with your spouse about past finances before getting married.
- While married keep separate accounts and one joint account.
- Have all joint credit card accounts closed
- Open new accounts in your name only
- Sell your car or house or have them refinanced

- Never remove your name from the title of the house
- Community states make you responsible

Chapter 8:

Building My Credit From the Ground Up

Cherrie's Story

I was in the leasing office paying for my rent one day, when the manager asked me, "How did you get your credit to be so good?" I told her, "Hard work, patience, and knowledge." She went on to say that her credit was not so good, but she desperately wanted to make sure that her daughter, who had just turned 18, established good credit and avoided the hardships that she'd had.

"Can you give me some tips?" she asked. "Actually, if your daughter wants to establish excellent credit, it takes strategy, and not just tips." A week later, I met with the manager and the daughter. I told the young girl to look for the credit card sales representatives in common areas and to apply for a student credit card. Despite having no credit, her chances of getting approved would be much higher since these cards are geared for students with no credit.

If she could not sign up for a student card, another option would be to borrow $500 from her mother to open a secured credit card. The bank would then use that deposit as collateral and issue her a credit card with a $500 limit. At this point, she would have to make her payments on time for six months to a year. The good thing about the secured card is that it would still allow her to apply for instant credit at large retailers like

Wal-Mart and Target. On this continued course and with payment consistency and reliability, she would easily develop excellent credit by the time she turned 21.

Both mother and daughter were astonished at how easy it was. The moral of the story is education is power, and if the girl had not sought counsel on building credit, she might have blindly applied for multiple credit cards, building up inquiries, and therefore, getting denied.

TAKE ACTION NOW!

Applying for multiple credit cards at one time is not the way to build credit when starting fresh. In doing this, you rack up multiple inquires on your credit report, which sends red flags to all potential lenders. As a result, you are denied and those inquires will stay on your credit report for two years. Whether you are trying to build or rebuild credit, you must select one credit building method and pay your bills on time for a year before applying for additional credit. This will show the bank that you have demonstrated your credit worthiness.

Can you tell me the various ways to build or rebuild my credit?

Yes. There are ways to establish or restore your credit. You can use a student credit card, the secured credit card, retail store cards, the credit unions rebuild your credit loan, secured bank loan, merchandise card, cosigner or a master and visa card.

What should I do first?

You want to get a copy of your credit report for review. Order your credit report using the methods discussed in chapter one. Once you have the credit report, review it for accounts that do not belong to you. If it's not clean, then use the dispute methods in chapter two on how to repair your credit report. If there is no incorrect information on your report, it's time to build or rebuild credit.

Tell me about the Student Credit Card?

This method is good for teenagers turning 18 and attending a community or a major university. This is the best time to get credit because banks are more lenient about approving college students. They don't worry about the students since they know that the parents will come to their rescue if they default on the loan. Because banks want to hook you in your early years, they have created two types of cards that are offered to students.

The first is the regular card, commonly offered to members of the public. The second is the student card, which is normally advertised on the college campuses and is sometimes mailed directly to the student. With the student card, the parents are required to cosign and the limit is no more than $1000, as these cards are good for students to practice the use of paying on time. Regular credit cards come with some type of gift, and you have to show proof that you are a student.

What about using a Secured Credit Card?

This method is good if you are trying to rebuild or start a new credit file. Getting a secured credit card and using it responsibly is an excellent way to build creditor's trust in your ability to use new credit, so that eventually, you can get an unsecured card. With a secured credit card, the companies require cardholders to secure their credit purchases by depositing a certain amount of money as collateral. That way, if you don't pay your secured credit card, the bank can get repaid by withdrawing the money you owe from the deposit you provided.

These cards can be used the same way as an unsecured card, except that your money secures them. The good thing about these cards is that no one knows that the card is secured. The downfall to these cards is that they usually come with high interest rates, over the limit fees, late fees, annual fees, start up fees, cash advance fees, and maintenance fees. This is the credit card company's way of encouraging you to pay in order to build your credit. Once you have reviewed your credit report and are ready to sign up for a secure card, consider the following:

- Ask the following questions before you sign a contract or send any money

- Does your company report to all three credit bureaus?

- When will I qualify for an unsecured line of credit?

- What are your credit card fees?

What is the best way to find secured cards?

- Talk with your major local banks and credit unions.
- Bankcard Holders of America at 524 Branch Dr. Salem, VA 24153
- Creditcards.com
- Creditcardscenter.com
- E-wisdom.com
- Lowermybills.com
- Banrate.com
- Cardrating.com

Banks known to issue secured cards with low limits

- Capitol One
- Orchard Bank
- New Millennium Bank

What about Retail Store Cards?

This method is good if you are building credit for the first time. Retail cards like those at Macy's and JCPenny's are easier to get than a major credit card. The reason the retail cards are easier to get is because they grant lower limits and the card is tied to merchandise in their store only. Apply for a card and then make your payments on time for six months. Pull your credit report and check your payment history.

How about the Credit Builder Loan - Credit Union?

This method is good if you are building or rebuilding your credit files. You know how important it is to have excellent credit. A Credit Builder Loan is your key to establishing or reestablishing your credit. Here's how it works. The Credit Union loans you money that is deposited into a certificate of deposit. You make regular payments that are reported to the credit-reporting agencies. Once the loan is paid off, you get the certificate of deposit and have a better credit score. The benefits of this program are that you don't have to put any money up front; the Credit Union reports to all three credit bureaus, and you establish a small saving at the end of the 12-month installment period.

Can I use a Secured Bank Loan?

This method is good if you are rebuilding or building credit for the first time. Save $500-$1000 and then visit various banks with your credit report in hand asking them whether they do secure passbook loans based on your savings. Once they agree, ask the loan officer if there is a prepayment penalty, what the interest rate is, and what credit bureaus they report to. Apply for a 12-month passbook loan, then with the loan from the first bank, go to another bank and open a second passbook loan with a 12-month pay period. Then wait three weeks and go to a third bank and repeat the process with the loan from the second bank. Now, you have three loans at three different banks for a 12-month payment plan. Now start making payments with the loan you received from the last bank. After six months of on time payments, check your credit report to make sure the loans are being reported correctly. Congratulations, you have just established superior credit with three bank installment loans.

Can I use a Merchandise Card to build Credit?

This method is used when you are rebuilding and building credit for the first time. Using a merchandise card could help you establish a high credit limit fast. Here is how it works. You apply for the merchandise card by buying $295 worth of e-books and music through the company's website (like Fingerhut, the catalog company). Once you have made your purchase, the organization will issue you a $5,000 line of credit to purchase more items. The best thing about this card is that they report to two of the major credit bureaus: Equifax and TransUnion. You also establish an instance credit trade line, which looks good on your credit report. In addition, there is no credit check, so you avoid having an inquiry on your report.

What about using a Cosigner?

This method is good when you are trying to build or establish credit. Talk with a family member or a friend to have them cosign for you since you don't have any credit. In addition, let them know that you are trying to build it. Cosigning means that due to your lack of credit or poor credit, the bank would like someone with good credit to back you up in case you default on the loan. Now, if you stop paying on the loan, the bank will go after your cosigner for the balance of the loan. Start with a small loan at the bank and make your payments on time for a year paying off the balance so that you can release your cosigner.

What is PRBC and how do I use this company to build credit?

PRBC is a non-traditional credit-reporting agency. They track the way you pay your rent, utilities, cable and cell phone bills. From there, they compile a payment history report that can be used as supplemental information along side with your credit report when lenders are trying to decide on whether to issue credit to you. FICO has partnered up with PRBC to provide Expansion scores based on your payment history with PRBC. These Expansion scores are only issued to the lenders upon request. In addition, all lenders do not use PRBC to consider your credit worthiness, so you must ask them to pull your PRBC report when applying for credit. In order to get started with PRBC, you can sign up with them and start reporting your good payment history from your rent, cable bills, utilities, and cell phone. PRBC will then charge you a small fee to verify your payment history and include it in your file. The good thing about PRBC is that your credit report with them is free, and you can get a copy at anytime. This method is best if you don't have any credit or a thin credit file.

When should I apply for a major Visa and Master Card?

This method is good after you have established at least two years of solid credit history. Your credit report should have one small credit card and one installment loan. With your mixture of credit trade lines and two years of a solid payment history, it's time to go for the big bank credit cards like Visa and Master card. The FICO scoring model really likes to see consumers with credit cards from the major banks. Go to one of your banks, like Bank of America, and ask them what type of credit score you would need to qualify for their Master card. Then apply to create AAA credit.

I just got rejected for credit, so what does a thin file mean?

It means that you do not have enough trade lines in your credit report to calculate a credit score or for a lender to evaluate your credit worthiness. People who are divorced, teenagers just turning 18, and immigrants all fall into the category of having thin files. FICO created a new way for consumer with a thin file to produce a credit score. It's called Expansion score, and it uses information from nontraditional sources to calculate a score. The program uses payday lenders, check monitoring companies, rent to own stores, utility information, and public records to help calculate a score.

What do creditors like to see on credit reports?

Make sure your credit report has your present employer, previous employment, residence, and phone number, since creditors like to see this information when you are applying for credit. They are checking for stability like how long you have been at your job and your home.

How long does it take to rebuild credit?

It can take from one to two years to build good credit if you follow the strategies presented to you in this chapter. You need to display at least one year of on time payments before major bank cards like American Express and Visa take you seriously.

How will paying with cash help me build credit?

Start getting into the habit of paying cash or paying with your debit card. Paying with cash helps you manage your budget, and it restricts you to the amount of things you can buy. If you can't afford it, don't buy it. In the long run, this will help you with management skills when it comes to paying down on your credit cards and personal debt. Use your debit card on emergency bases only. Debit cards can cost you with over the limit fees and insufficient fund fees if you don't track your spending.

How many credit cards do I need?

Carry one to two bankcards, one retail card and one gasoline card. Creditors want to see how you will manage more than one card as far as payment history goes. If you can't pay the minimum monthly payment every month, don't use most of the cards.

What if I had a bankruptcy?

You can start rebuilding in 18 to 20 months.

I'm a foreigner and now I live in the USA with no credit?

Continue using your International credit card, and then get a letter from the bank in your country displaying your good payment history. Take that letter to your local bank loan officer and apply for a loan using the letter as a reference.

What is piggybacking?

Have a friend or family member with good credit call up their credit card company and have them add you to their account as an authorized user. The credit card company will issue a card in your name, and once the card arrives at your friend's house. He or she will cut the card up. Wait a month later and check your credit report to see if your friends entire credit history for that card is on your credit report. This is a fast way to build credit within 30 days. Now, the downfall to this method is that if your friend makes a late payment or refuses to pay, your credit report will show the same negative activity, therefore damaging your good credit rating. Do consider the potential consequences carefully before moving in this direction. In addition, FICO 08 model has eliminated this method for calculating your credit score, so the technique may or may not work, but it is still worth a try.

How can I add new accounts to my credit reports?

The first step you can take in strengthening your credit situation is to write to the credit agencies and request that they add your good accounts if they do not appear on your credit report. Since the main purpose behind adding accounts to your credit report is to strengthen your report, you only want to add accounts that are deemed to have a perfect paying history.

Normally, utility companies and cell phone companies do not report your payment history to the credit bureaus, but if you write them a letter requesting that they add your good payment history to your credit report, they might grant your request. If, for some reason, they do not add your account, get copies of your payment history and submit copies to the credit bureaus yourself. Credit bureaus don't have to add this information, but they will place it on your report for a fee.

What companies do not report to the credit bureaus?

Some travel entertainment companies, gasoline companies, local retailers, and credit unions are among those creditors who don't report to the credit bureaus.

How often should I use my credit card?

Creditors like to see that you can make your payments on time, so if you have a credit card, use it to buy small items, then pay off the balance to avoid interest fees monthly.

What do you mean show the positive?

When applying for credit, emphasize why the credit should be granted. It is important to capitalize on your strong points by making them the focus of your credit strategy. A good income history is one of the strongest points you can make. An excellent track record with credit bureaus, with your banking institution, and with creditors (such as the telephone company and utilities) goes a long way toward making you look good. Lenders like to see evidence of earning power over a long period of time, as well as a consistent record of making payments on time.

Why should I educate myself?

The credit repair system is extremely intricate and is constantly changing. Year-by-year millions of Americans suffer from bad credit and get themselves deeper into debt. To guard yourself against costly mistakes, I encourage you to read as many books as you can on credit repair and personal finance so that you can learn the various ways to improve your credit.

How do I stay out of trouble?

When rebuilding credit, you want to strictly limit the amount of credit you apply for. Shop for deals on the best credit cards or loans out there. Get credit for a specific purpose and not just to have it. By keeping the limits low and limiting the amount of credit you obtain, it will be easier for you to make your payments on time and keep your limits reduced. This is how you build your credit step-by-step.

How can I buy a house with no credit or poor credit?

Most banks will not lend to you while you are trying to rebuild your credit, but there are two other secret ways you can buy a house with bad credit. The first is by buying owner-financed homes. Some homeowners are willing to finance their home without a credit check, as they are acting as the bank. Second, you can rent to own. Put down a large down payment and establish a leasing agreement with the owner. In this contract, you agree to pay the landlord monthly payments for up to two years. When the agreement is over, you will have the option of buying the home or moving out. If you decide to buy, your credit will be solid by this time, and you can go back to the bank for a loan.

If I buy a car, will it help me build credit?

Yes. Most major cities have car dealers who offer bad credit car loans, though they do come with a price, entailing a large down payment and a high interest rate. Before you sign the loan agreement, make sure the dealership reports your payment history to the credit bureaus. Look at used car dealers who will finance cars with no credit as long as you have a good job and a down payment. Watch out for "buy here, pay here" dealers as they charge high interest rates and hit you with extras like extended warranties. The good thing about financing a car loan is that it shows up as an installment loan and adds a mixture of credit on your credit report.

Why should I monitor my credit reports?

During the rebuilding stages, it's important that you check your credit reports every four months for inaccurate information that might damage your credit. Common errors to look out for are:

- Accounts that are not yours
- Inaccurate balances
- Wrong date of last activity
- Incorrect credit limit listed
- Unauthorized inquires
- Incorrect personal information
- Inaccurate amounts listed
- Wrong account number
- Wrong original creditor
- Incorrect charge off date

What are the benefits of joining a credit union?

These banks have better rates on credit cards, car loans and personal loans. Their qualification requirements are less strict, they are more forgiving than banks, and people with bankruptcies may qualify for their loans. When looking for a credit union, ask your current employer or school, or search the Internet or yellow pages for a good place to start.

Key points to remember

- Use the various methods to build credit
- Use the student card
- Try the secured card
- Look into the retail store cards
- Talk with credit unions.

Chapter 9:

Raising My Credit Score

Troy's Story

While I was driving in my car, my brother called me up for advice on how to raise his credit score. I asked him what he thought the problem was, and he said that every time he applied for new credit he would get denied even though he felt his credit was good. I asked him when was the last time he looked at his credit report. He said it had been a while. We couldn't do much without having a copy of his report as a starting point, so I asked him to print up a copy so that we could find the problem.

Two days later, I met up with Troy. I looked at his credit report and discovered that there were a couple of accounts on the report that were not his, and it was these two accounts that were bringing his score down. I also, noticed that he was maxed out on most of his small limit credit cards. I told him that he needed to start disputing the items on his report and start working on bringing his balances down.

One month later, Troy called me and stated that with my advice, he could get the negative items off of his credit report. In addition, he had also reduced his credit card balances to 35% with the help of a second job. As a result, he could get the American Express card he was trying to get for months. The moral of the story is education is power. If Troy had not reduced his balances or checked his credit report for errors, he wouldn't have gotten approved for the American Express card.

TAKE ACTION NOW!

Not understanding the five elements that make up your FICO score could have a tremendous negative effect on you getting approved for credit. For example, if you are 30 days late within the first two years of having an account, this could bring your credit score down by 30 points. In return, you could get denied for a home loan based on that single 30 day late indication. In today's society, your credit score is used whenever you apply for credit, so it's important that you understand how to raise it and maintain it. Monitoring the five areas of your credit score will let you know which areas need improvement.

What is a FICO score?

A FICO score is a three-digit number that is built from the information contained in your credit report. It summarizes information like your payment history, the amount of debt you carry, the length of your credit history, the amount of new credit you applied for, and the type of trade lines you have in your report.

How do I start a score?

To get a score, you need one account on your file for six months, and one trade line updated in the past six months.

What is a good score?

Lenders say with a 700-720 score you get the best prime rates. With a 620, you get the sub prime riskier rates.

- 750-850 - Excellent
- 660-749 - Good
- 620-659 - Fair
- 350-619 - Poor

Where can I get my score?

You can get your score from various online companies, but it won't be your true FICO score because the organizations are not pulling their scores from the FICO model. These scores will only give you a close indication of what your numbers are. Only order your credit score from MYFICO.COM because most lenders use them when making a decision to grant you credit. When looking at your score, pay attention to the middle number because these are the numbers lenders focus on. You can also pull your score from all three credit bureaus, though they use their own model to calculate your credit score.

How is my score calculated?

It's calculated by your payment history, the amount you owe, the length of your credit, what new credit have you applied for, and the type of trade lines you have.

Payment history

Your paying habits are 35% of your credit score. If your late payments are recent, it will lower your score more than if you were behind in the past. In addition, a 90-day late indication will severely damage your score over a 30-day mark. In addition, public records like tax liens, judgments, and bankruptcies fall into the same category and could take your score down even further, so make sure you are current with the creditors and always pay your bills on time.

Amount you owe

The balance on your accounts is 30% of your available credit score, so using all of your credit will worry lenders and hurt your score. The lower your balance, the better your score.

Length of credit

The amount of time you've had your credit makes up 15% of your credit score. The age on your trade lines is very important to lenders because it shows that you have paid your bills on time. Reliability and longevity are good traits for additional credit.

New credit

This makes up 10% of your score. The FICO model looks at how many accounts you've applied for lately, any fresh accounts you have opened. The model looks at time passed since you requested for new credit, and the amount of time since you opened another account. If you open too many accounts in a short period of time, you will look desperate to the lenders, and they don't like loaning money to needy customers.

Type of credit you use

This section makes up 10% of your score. FICO wants to see a healthy mix of trade lines like a couple of bank cards, retail store cards, and installment loans like a car, personal or a mortgage loan.

How can I improve my credit score?

Pull your credit report

You can start by removing errors from your credit report. While scanning your credit report, look for any inquiries that you did not authorize. Inquiries could lower your score as much as five points per inquiry. Get the creditor to prove that you gave them permission to pull your credit report, and if they can't prove it, then the inquiry must be deleted according to the law. You should also inspect your report for the following:

- Accounts that are not yours
- Trade lines that are incorrect
- Outdated debts
- Accounts with the mark of authorized user
- Credit accounts that were paid but still shows outstanding
- Credit limits that are not being reported
- Any errors that require dispute
- Unauthorized Inquiries

Know who is looking at your credit report

When you give your social security number out on applications, you are giving the creditor permission to look at your credit report, but you have to watch it to see if unauthorized users are looking at it too.

Contact the creditor

When disputing an item on your credit report, you should not only contact the credit bureaus but also the creditor. Make the creditor prove that you were late as they are reporting it to the credit bureaus. If they can't prove that you were late, ask them to delete the negative item and this can improve your score.

Keep your address updated with the credit bureaus

If you move, make sure you notify all of your creditors with your new address. If you don't and you miss your statement, late fees will be added, which could cause you to go over your limit. If you fail to make the payment within the 30 days, the creditor will report you to the credit bureaus and your score will take a deep hit.

Pay your bills on time

Make a list of all of your debts and their due dates. Then type in the due dates into your computer and cell phone calendars with reminders made active. Use the Internet banking program, and your online credit card site to send you email reminders when your bills are due. In addition, you can set up your accounts to have the money automatically taken out at the due date. When paying your bills, you can pay them as they come in, use online banking or bill pay or through your financial institution web site. Using the various methods mentioned above will help you pay your debts. Making each payment on time raises your credit score.

Pay down your debt

Put your debts in order from the card with the highest balance to the lowest. Pay each account down to 30% and keep it there to increase your score. Finding money to help you pay down your debt may be difficult, but there are numerous ways to raise extra cash. You can have a garage sale, sell on Ebay, get an extra job, pull from your savings, borrow from friends, and cut your expenses. Any of these are an option.

Don't close old accounts

Closing trade lines won't help. In fact, it will hurt your score by reducing your total available credit and making your balances seem higher. It also makes your total credit look young, and the FICO model likes to see age on accounts because of payment history. Last, you want to keep the cards active by having a monthly bill debited from your card at the end of the month to avoid the creditor from closing your account due to lack of use.

Ask for a credit increase

Ask your creditor to raise your limit that way it will reduce your balance and give you a slight bump up in your score.

Apply for credit sparingly

Don't apply for many accounts in a short period of time because the credit bureau will send a Trans Alert to the creditors informing them that you have applied for multiple accounts.

Re-aging

Ask your creditor to re-age your account to improve your credit score. This method is the process by which your creditor agrees to forgive your late payment history and reclassify your account as up to date. You must qualify for re-aging according to (FFIEC) Federal Financial Examination Council and must establish and follow a policy that requires you to demonstrate a renewed willingness and ability to repay the debt. The account must be at least nine months old, and you must make three consecutive minimum monthly payments.

Rapid re-score

In this method, the lender will review your credit report and tell you which item needs to be paid off or fixed. You will then pay off the negative items and get proof from the creditor. You then give the proof to the lender who will give it to the third party vender who passes the information to the credit bureau. The bureau will then update your credit report reflecting your new credit score. This strategy is used primarily when you are trying to get a home. This feature is offered by a third party vender, and the company is contracted by the credit bureau, not to offer the service to the public, but only to mortgage brokers.

Your credit score

A credit score of 720 opens the doors to all credit, and a score of 500 closes the door to all credit. A 620 gets you qualified and a 660 opens the door to additional programs.

Have the credit bureaus add new accounts

Ask the credit bureau to add any account with a payment history that is not reflecting on your credit report.

Don't pay off old debt

Paying off outdated negative bills can actually hurt your score by renewing the date of the last activity of the debt and making it current.

Your true credit card balance

If you know that your credit card balance is lower than what the credit bureau is showing, write the credit card company, and have them update your credit card balance with the credit bureaus, so that your score will increase.

Applying for a car or a mortgage

If you are planning to buy a new car or a house within six months, then don't apply for new credit, which can lower your score and stop you from getting the car or house.

Don't apply for a retail store charge card just to get the discount

If you apply for a retail store card, you will lower your score in three ways. First, retail cards have low limits, and if you buy an item that will push your card to the max, it will lower your score. Second, when you open a new account, it will lower the total age on the rest of your cards. Third, it will produce a hard inquiry, which can lower your score by five points.

Ask them to remove the late entry

This technique is good if you have a long history with the creditor and have not been delinquent more than two times. Write a letter to the credit card company on a professional letterhead explaining that you are loyal to the company, and that you would like their assistance in removing a few late entries on your credit report.

Check the company out on the net

Before sending money to a company or buying an item on the Internet, review the company's history with the complaint board and Better Business Bureau. Never send a check. Instead send a money order so that you don't have to expose your checking account number.

Check your credit report and score on a regular basis

You can check it once or three times a year, but it is best to check it every four months. If someone steals your identity and open accounts in your name, call the credit bureaus and asked them to put either a 90-day or a seven-year fraud alert (a notification by the creditor when someone tries to open an account in your name) in your file. You can even place a credit freeze (the creditor or lender can't pull your credit report without your permission) on your account. When you are a victim of Identity theft, the law allows you to get a free credit report from all three bureaus.

Inquiries

Be careful not to get too many credit card inquires because it could drop your score. The banks don't like to see that you have applied for credit all around the town. If you are applying for a car loan or a mortgage within 45 days, it will count as one inquiry. Soft inquires won't hurt your score, but hard ones will. Be careful when you search online comparing car quotes because some credit bureaus may count the inquiries against you.

Don't lie on your loan application

Don't lie to improve your credit score for the following reasons: First, banks can check your correct score with no problem. And second, it's fraud if you misrepresent information on a credit card application.

Budgeting

Budgeting is a major factor in why people have a bad credit score. Spend time formulating a weekly and monthly budget. It will allow you to spend less than you earn and put extra money away toward paying off your debt.

Savings

Try to save each month for emergencies. By saving, you will avoid over-extending your credit cards, which can bring your credit score down. Start out with saving 5% of your income every month and then go to 10%. You can have your bank take the money out every month and have it transferred to your savings.

Building Assets

It can help you improve your credit score by allowing you to apply for secure credit lines using your assets as collateral.

Plan for a financial emergency

Emergencies such as losing your job, a medical crisis, or a death in the family can often be an unexpected financial strain, if you're unprepared. You must have money in place to maintain your bills, or your credit score could take a hit because all of your available money will go toward your emergency.

Get the right insurance to help with emergencies

Get life insurance, health insurance, disability insurance, and car insurance. If you have an emergency in any of these areas and you don't have proper coverage, you can find yourself in serious debt and with a damaged credit score.

Marriage and your credit score

If you are married and you and your spouse decide to get a divorce, joint accounts can bring your credit score down if one of you does not pay the bill. Even if you've gone to court and have legally decided who will be responsible for each bill, the only thing that matters to your creditors is that one of you send your payment on time. According to the credit card companies, both parties are liable for the debt.

Know how money works

Learn the in and outs of how money works for you, so that you can be better prepared to pay your bills. You should also read books on money, budgets, and attend seminars.

Staying in financial shape

When applying for loans, a lender will look at your savings, your income and your employment. You want to make sure that you keep a good amount of savings in your account to show the lender that you have the discipline when it comes to handling money. They will also look at your income to see whether you make enough money to keep up with the monthly payments. Finally, they will look at the length of employment to make sure that you are stable. The above factors will help you get a loan, which will help you raise your score in the long run.

Late fees removed

If you are late, ask the lender to waive the late fee as a courtesy because most lenders will do that for you if you have not used all of your late waivers for the year. Lending institutions allow either one or two late fee waivers yearly. Then take the money that they were going to charge you and reduce the balances on your credit cards for an increase in your credit score.

Stay organized with your bills

Get a file cabinet to track your bills and place them in an area where you can get to them quickly. Know the date of your payments and use calendars to remind you of your due dates. Take advantage of automatic payment deduction and electronic email reminders from creditors when offered.

Set goals

Set goals to track your credit repair efforts. For example, create a tracking list for your credit repair letters. Note whom you send letters out to and when. Set up reminders to check your score regularly to see whether it has improved. Create dates on when you are going to pay off your debt and recheck your score.

Loans and your credit score

Loans affect your credit score more than any other item on your credit report. The type of loan, the amount you owe, and your payment history can destroy or improve your credit.

Refinancing your home loan or your car loan

Refinancing can help and hurt your credit score. It can help your score because you will be able to reduce your monthly payment and get a lower interest rate since your credit score has improved. It can hurt your score because of new inquires that hit your credit report, and opening and closing accounts.

Bad credit lenders

My first advice is to stay away from these types of lenders, but if you are in a bind and you need to repair your credit by showing the banks that you can make payments on time, then getting a loan from a bad credit lender may be the thing you need to do. When you get these loans be aware that the interest rate will be four or five times higher than the normal loan interest rate, but you can always refinance the loan once your credit score has improved.

While on vacation or in the hospital

During a vacation or a long stay in the hospital, you have to make arrangements to have your bills paid. You can pay your bills in advance or designate one of your friends or family members to do it for you to avoid your credit score from being damaged.

College student and credit

Most students who attend college tend to build up debt before they graduate, but this can be stopped with a little education. Students on their way to debt and a bad credit score need to see their Financial Aid office for help. This office has information on credit counseling, scholarships, budgeting, books on money, personal finance workshops, and tax filing information.

Raise your credit score by consolidating your loan

If you have a number of loans and credit cards, and you may be missing some of your payments each month. Not keeping up with your payments will cause your credit score to go down. Consolidation can make this problem disappear. It consists of taking out one loan to pay off all of your smaller loans. In addition, you will also only have one consolidated payment to keep track of per month.

Key points to remember

- A FICO score is 700-740 is your target
- Always order your score from Myfico.com
- Dispute negative items on your credit report
- Pay down your balances
- Pay on time
- Don't close old accounts
- Don't lie on your application
- Have the credit bureau remove unauthorized inquires

Chapter 10:

Should I File For

Bankruptcy?

Karen's Story

While I was having dinner with my wife, she mentioned a friend that was having financial problems and said that she was considering bankruptcy. I asked how much debt she had accrued, and offered to provide a credit analysis for her to evaluate her situation before she filed for bankruptcy. Shortly after, my wife called her friend to set up the meeting. During the meeting, I talked with her friend, Karen, about how she could fix her credit report, negotiate with creditors, raise her score, and rebuild her credit. We discussed the advantages and disadvantages to bankruptcy, and concluding the meeting, she decided it wasn't for her. Karen decided instead to use some of the techniques I had discussed with her in the meeting. The moral of the story is that education is power. If Karen had listened to her friends, she may have filed for a bankruptcy that she didn't even need, her credit would have been destroyed, and the negative marks on her record would have left their stain much longer.

TAKE ACTION NOW!

Many consumers feel that bankruptcy is their only option once their debt is so deep they can no longer pay basic bills like food and rent. Because of the abuse of bankruptcy, Congress has passed strict qualification laws for bankruptcy. But filing for bankruptcy is not always your first options to getting out of debt. There are many organizations that will help you get out of debt if you are willing to seek them out for help.

Why do most people consider bankruptcy?

Consumers think about bankruptcy when they carry a debt load that far exceeds their annual income, and they feel that there is no way out of the situation. This usually occurs when you go through a divorce, become really ill, and you can't work, or you lose your job.

Should I file bankruptcy?

Only when you have exhausted all of your available avenues such as talking with your credit card company, car, and mortgage lenders and your student loan representative about the various options you have to explore. You should also look into Consumer credit counseling organizations, debt consolidation, balance transfers and taping your savings and investments. If none of these options worked, and your debt exceeds your annual salary, then it's time to talk with a bankruptcy lawyer. Moreover, you must look at your advantages and disadvantages to filing.

Credit cards

Talk with your lender and see if any of the following options are available.

- Having your interest and payments reduced
- Changing your payment dates
- Qualifying for a hardship program

- Suspend payments until you get caught up
- Settling your debts for 20% on the dollar

Car

Before you get too behind on your car payment, see if the bank will let you do any of the following:

- Move your late payments to the end of your loan
- Refinance the car for a lower payment and interest rate
- Participate in a hardship program

Home

Talk with your lender to see if they can help you in any way. You can also do the following:

- Try to get your payments reduced or suspended
- Contact your local housing authority for help
- Try refinancing
- Selling the home

Student Loan

Since the student loan can't be discharged in bankruptcy, talk with a representative at the student loan center and try some of the following options:

- Request a deferment
- Apply for a forbearance
- See if you qualify for the income sensitive program

- Look into the pay interest only options for a certain amount of time

Consumer Credit Counseling

Schedule an appointment with credit consumer counselor. The CCC is a non-profit organization that assists consumers who are in financial trouble. Here is what they will do for you:

- Help sort out your financial problems

- Provide credit education

- Help you with a budget

- Provide you with a plan to get out of debt

- Set up a payment plan for you

- Negotiate with creditors on your behalf

- Reduce interest rates and get late fees removed

You can reach them at www.consumercounseling.org or 202- 637-4851

These organizations also assist consumers with their debt load:

Institute of Consumer Financial Education at www.ICFE.info or 602-239-1401

National foundation for credit Counseling www.nfcc.org or 800-388-2227

Debtors Anonymous www.debtorsanonymous.org or 781-453-2743

Debt consolidation

You may be able to lower your credit cards and loan debt by consolidating through a second mortgage or a home equity loan. With a second mortgage, consumers take out a loan against their equity in their home but this comes with advantages and disadvantages. Line of credit is very similar to the home equity loan but instead of getting all of your money at one time, you get a debit card with a certain amount of money on it. You can use the money whenever you need it.

Home equity loan

Positives

- The loan comes with a fixed interest rate
- Interest could be tax deductible

Negatives

- You could lose your house if you default on the loan
- Interest rates you pay will be higher than the interest rates on your home loan

Line of credit

Positives

- You get the money as you need it
- A debt card is offered so that you can use it like a credit card

Negatives

- Variable interest rates meaning the rates could change at any time
- Easy access to the debit card

Balance Transfer

If you have a lot of credit cards, seek out credit card companies with lower interest rates and see whether you can move your card balance to this new card. Talk with the bank on how to qualify. After transferring all of your high interest cards, take the money saved to help pay down your debt.

Savings and Investments

Cashing out our savings can be a difficult thing to do since it took you a long time to build it. If the savings is not making you any money, it's best to deplete most of it and pay off your high interest credit cards. Leave enough in your account to cover emergencies. In addition, if you have a 401k, you can borrow against it to assist you with your debt.

What are the advantages and disadvantages to filing bankruptcy?

Advantages?

- You get a new start
- Stop Collection calls, judgments, and wage garnishments.
- You get credit education
- You will start getting credit again after one year
- Most of your debts will be discharged

Disadvantages?

- It destroys your credit for 10 years
- You can't stop taxes, child support, or student loans
- Your credit score drops by a 100 to 150 points
- You can't borrow money for at least a year
- Renting an apartment becomes harder
- Insurance rates go up
- Employers may look at you differently
- Higher interest rates
- Higher insurance rates

Tell me about chapter 7 and 13?

Chapter 7 Bankruptcy

Chapter 7 known as a liquidation bankruptcy is the most common form of bankruptcy. When filing, you may have to give up some of your assets, like your car, house, and other items depending on what your exemption laws are in your state. Each state allows you to keep certain assets when you file bankruptcy. If you file Chapter 7 it will discharge most of your debts except for Federal and State taxes, student loans, child support and alimony. During your bankruptcy, you will still be able to receive social security, disability, unemployment benefits, and your pension.

Chapter 13 Bankruptcy

With a Chapter 13-wage-earner bankruptcy, you can keep your assets and pay back what you can. You will also work on your debts and make payments for two to five years. Every creditor gets a portion of their owed debt, and that is why some people say Chapter 13 looks better on their credit report because in Chapter 7 creditors get nothing. Chapter 13 allows you to keep your house, and it stops collection harassment and lawsuits.

What is the new bankruptcy law?

In 2005, lenders persuaded congress to pass The Bankruptcy Abused Prevention and Consumer Protection Act, which is a law to help cut down on consumers abusing the bankruptcy law. Under this new law, you have to pass a means test to be eligible for Chapter 7.

What is a means test and the education requirements?

To pass the means test your net income has to be below the median income in your state. If your income is above the median for your state, you won't qualify. If you are eligible, you must go through a credit-counseling course six months before filing. Then, during the proceedings, you must take a personal finance course and turn in your completion certificate before your debt can be discharged.

Where can I find the means income standards?

www.usdoj.gov

www.justice.gov/ust/eo/bapcpa/meanstesting.htm

What about approved credit consumer counselors?

www.greenpathbk.com

www.cccsatl.org

Where can I find exemption laws and a bankruptcy attorney?

www.bankruptcyaction.com/nvexemptions.htm
www.bankruptcyinformation.com

Key points to remember

- Exhaust all options before filing
- Understand your advantages and disadvantages
- Understand the difference between a Chapter 7 and 13

Chapter 11:

Suing the Credit Bureaus to get items removed from my credit report

Mike's Story

I was sitting in court waiting for a representative to call my name for Jury duty. While waiting, there was a man named Mike sitting next to me. He asked me what I was reading and I replied, "Just some notes on credit repair." We started to talk the usual credit subjects: debt, negative marks, and credit bureaus. But Mike piqued my interest when he told me that he had recently tried to get an account off of his credit report due to identity theft, but the credit bureau refused to remove it.

I told Mike that he certainly had grounds for a lawsuit case against the credit bureau, and that he could do so in a small claims court. First, I advised Mike to write a complaint to the Federal Trade Commission and a request to the credit bureau asking them to delete the error. When these formal complaints and requests did not work, Mike wrote back to the bureau informing them that he was seeking legal advice and requesting (a second time) for them to delete the negative item. With enough documentation of the credit bureau's refusal to investigate his claim and remove the negative item, Mike was able to file a suit in small claims court.

Once filed, the process server served the credit bureaus with the complaint. Seven days later, the credit bureaus sent Mike an updated credit report minus the disputed items. The moral of the story is education is power. If Mike hadn't known that he could sue the credit bureaus for violating the FCRA, those negative items would still be on his credit report damaging his score and preventing him from buying the house of his dreams.

TAKE ACTION NOW!

Collection agencies, creditors, and credit bureaus know that most consumers will not sue them in court because of the time and expense required. As a result, agencies often take advantage of the average person by violating the consumer laws put in place to protect you. However, with a little knowledge on how the law and the small claims court system work, you can turn the big agencies bad ways against them and make them follow the law.

Suing the creditor

You are well within your rights to sue the creditor if they violate any of the following laws under the FCRP/FDCPA:

First cause of action

If a creditor reports your credit history inaccurately, you can sue them for defamation, and financial injury. See US Court of Appeals, Ninth Circuit, No. 00-15946, Nelson vs. Chase Manhattan for precedent. This violation carries a fine of $1,000.00 per violation.

Second cause of action

If you dispute a debt with the creditor, and they fail to report the dispute to the credit bureaus, they will be in violation of Section 623, which carries a fine of $1,000 per violation.

Third cause of action

If the creditor pulls your credit report without your permission, you can sue for injury to your credit report and credit score, which carries a fine of $1,000.00. (FRA Section 604 (A)(3).

Suing the credit bureau

The credit bureau can also be sued for any of the following causes:

First cause of action

If the credit bureau refused to correct information on your credit report after being provided with proof, you can sue them for defamation and willful injury. (FCRA Section 623). Recovery-extent of damages incurred by the wronged party, as deemed by the courts.

Second cause of action

If the credit bureaus reinsert a removed item from your credit report without notifying you in writing within five business days, you can sue them for violating FCRA Part (A)(5)(B) which carries a fine of $1000.00.

Third cause of action

If the credit bureaus fail to respond to your written disputes within 30 days, a 15-day extension may be granted if they receive information from the creditor within the first 30 days, you can sue them for violating FCRA Section 611 Part (A)(1) which carries a fine of $1000 per violation.

Fourth cause of action

If a creditor or credit bureau tries to re-age your account by updating the date of last activity on your credit report in the hopes of keeping negative information on your account longer, you can sue them for violating FCRA Section 605, which carries a fine of $1000.00 per violation.

Suing collection agencies

Collection agencies can also be sued for violating the Fair Debt Practice Act or any of the following actions:

First cause of action

If you dispute a debt with the collection agency, and they fail to notify the credit bureau of your dispute, they can be sued for violating Section 807 (8), which carries a fine of $1,000.00.

Second cause of action

If the collection agency does not validate your debt yet continues to report the negative item on your credit report, they can be sued for violating Section 809 (b), which carries a fine of $1,000.00.

Third cause of action

If you sent the collection agency a cease and desist letter, and they still call you, they will be in violation of Section 805 (c), which carries a fine of $1,000.00.

Fourth cause of action

If a collection agency tries to re-age your account by updating the date of last activity on your credit report in the hopes of keeping negative information on your account longer, you can sue them for violating FCRA Section 605, which carries a fine of $1000.00 per violation.

Fifth cause of action

If they do not validate your debt yet continue to pursue collection activity (e.g. file for a judgment, call or write you) they will be in violation of the FDCPA, which carries a fine of $1,000.

Sixth cause of action

If the collection agency cashes a post dated check before the date on the cash date, costs you money by making you accept collect calls or COD mail, or takes or threatens to take any personal property without a judgment, they will be in violation of the FDCPA which carries a fine of $1,000 for every violation.

Seventh cause of action

If the collection agency calls you before 8am, or after 9PM, calls you at work when the collectors know your boss prohibits it, calls a third party and tells them about your debt, harasses or verbally abuses you, or claims that they will garnish your wages, seize your property, or have you arrested, they will be in violation of the FDCPA which carries a fine of 1,000 for each violation.

What is small claims court?

It's an informal, inexpensive procedure to handle a claim. In this court, the plaintiff (you) and the defendant (the credit bureau, collection agency, or creditor) argue a cause of action in front of a judge that can produce a monetary award in between $100 to $10,000 depending on the state court. The benefits to filing in small claims court are as follows:

- You don't need an attorney
- The case is short
- You represent yourself
- You don't need any legal training
- There is a small amount of paperwork involved
- Rules of the court are simple

What are the powers of a small claims court?

In the small claims court, the judge can award claims for money such as out of pocket losses directly related to the subject matter of the suit. For example, you can be awarded the cost of the suit. These include the filing fees, sheriff's fees, and witness fees. The judge can also order the defendant to pay punitive damages if he violated a state or federal statute, and it allows damages. The judge, however, cannot issue out rulings on specific performance (making someone comply with a contract clause) or injunction relief (stopping something from happening).

What is a court of Equity?

These courts have the power to order a company to complete a specific performance. If you are trying to get an item removed from your credit report, and you sue the credit bureau in a court of equity, you have a good chance of getting it removed. The reason for this is the credit bureau/creditor/collection agency won't show up, and you get a default judgment. Now, if you are suing for monetary damages, the credit bureau may file a motion to have the case moved to Federal court. In this case, you would have to hire an attorney. Before filing your claim, ask the clerk of court if the court is a court of equity.

What type of cases can be heard?

Any type of case involving a small amount of money can be heard. The small claims courts have limits on how much you can sue for, and if your claim is over that limit, you must hire a lawyer and sue in a higher court.

Who can I sue?

Any person or business that currently resides, works, or does business in your state. You must, however, be able to provide a current address (not a P.O. BOX) for the defendant. Talk with the clerk of the court to make sure that the defendant's address is in the right district. Moreover, you want to make sure you have the credit bureau or collection agencies correct name to avoid the case from being dismissed based on a technicality.

How can I find my court?

In every county, there are small claims courts. You can look in the yellow pages, call the local operator, or do a search on the Internet for the small claims court in your county. Once you locate the court, talk with the clerk to make sure you have the right court.

Do I need a lawyer?

In most small claims courts, attorneys are not allowed, so you won't need a lawyer. However, you should still seek legal advice if you plan on suing the credit bureau or a collection agency. When talking with a lawyer, ask questions about the procedures, the law, counter claims, evidence, your defenses and the possible outcome. Go to prepaidlegal.com and sign up for a membership. Once you have selected a lawyer, you can have him or her review your case for as low as $17 a month.

Where can I find an attorney?

- You can go to legal clinics put on by law schools
- Go to your local legal aid office
- Go to the clerk of the court (only for small claims procedures)
- Look through the yellow pages or legal newspapers
- Consult a bar association referral service
- Check a local law library
- Prepaidlegal.com

Once you have selected a lawyer, have him or her review your argument and facts. If you are suing for an amount higher than the small claims court limit, you will need an attorney that will work on a contingency bases, meaning he will not charge you up front but will take a percentage from your award if you win the case.

Can I collect attorney fees in small claims court?

Some states allow you to collect attorney fees and others do not. Talk with counsel or check with your small claims court on this matter.

Can I sue in small claims court under the federal law?

Yes, if your state does not have a law that regulates the credit bureaus. Be aware that the credit bureau may try to get the lawsuit moved to Federal Court since it's a Federal law that you are suing them under. If this happens, you will need to hire an attorney.

What is the statute of limitation for filing a lawsuit?

The statute is two years from the date of the violation for the credit bureau and one year for the collection agency, so make sure you file your claim before the statute expires.

Do I have a case?

First, check with your local attorney general's office and the office of consumer affairs to see whether your state has credit reporting laws that you can sue under. If the state does not have any laws, you can look through your records to see if the bureau has violated Federal law.

How will I prove my case?

You can prove your case by showing the judge that the credit bureau or the collection agency has willfully violated the law by failing to comply with the statutes. To support your case, you will need the evidence you've gathered. Evidence may be wide-ranging, including letters to and from the bureaus, recordings, certified return receipts, witnesses, even notes taken in a journal regarding conversations held with the collection agency or credit bureau. You can also use other court cases to support your argument.

What must I show during my lawsuit?

You must show that you were harmed in some way due to the credit bureau's willful non-compliance. For example, if you were turned down for a home loan, if your interest rates on your other credit cards went up, or if you were denied a job based on the negative marks in your credit report, their refusal or negligence in cooperating to remove the negative marks will have led to harmful developments.

Should I try to settle first?

Sending a demand letter to the credit bureau or the collection agency and trying to settle your claim before going to court presents you in a very respectable light before the judge. Allow the credit bureau or the collection agency 10 days to respond to your letter, and if there is no response, file a copy of the letter and the certified return receipt with the court as proof that you tried to settle. In your letter, you should ask for changes to your credit report and for punitive damages for violating the law.

How do I find cases?

You can either go to your public law library or use online legal research databases like westlaw.com or lexisnexis.com or www.versuslaw.com or www.jurisearch.com. Once you are at your public law library, ask the librarian for assistance on researching cases similar to your argument. A legal encyclopedia is the best place to start your research because they are indexed, organized, covers a broad spectrum of problems, and a good source to see how courts responded to cases like yours.

How should I prepare before filing the claim?

You should take a trip down to your small claims court and sit in on a few cases just to see the procedure. Take notes on how long it takes to present each case, type of interaction with the judge, the type of proof presented, even the appropriate manner of dress for court.

How do I file a claim?

Every court has different procedures, so go online to your small claims court and review their filing instructions. There will be a fee, which is based off of the amount you are suing for. This fee is due at the time of your filing. You can pay by cash, credit, debit card, money order, or cashier check. The claim can be filed in person, or at the after hour drop box or by mail, and all documents should be typed or written clearly.

What happens after the claim is filed?

After the claim is filed, you are assigned a case number and a court date which will be set out to be heard in 90 to 120 days from the filing date.

What is the basis of my claim?

You should have the following elements covered explicitly in your claim:

- Who is your defendant? (The credit bureau, collection agency, or creditor?)

- Describe the circumstances. (What happened?)

- What law was violated? (FCRA or the FDCPA?)

- What is the value of your losses? (How much money did you lose?)

- How were you injured? (By not being able to qualify for a loan? Through increased credit card interest rates?)

Who serves the credit bureau with the complaint?

Anyone not affiliated with the case may serve the credit bureau, but you are responsible for having the complaint served. Once you file, the complaint has to be served right away, and proof of delivery must be filed with the court 10 days from the court hearing date. You can use a sheriff, a third party not involved in the case, or a process server. You can also send it by mail with a certified return receipt. When mailing, make sure you ask for restrictive delivery, meaning a register agent for the company needs to sign for the complaint and check with your court for serving procedures.

How do I find the register agent (a representative of the company) for the credit bureau or the collection agency?

Go to the Secretary of State website where the company is based, and do a name search. If the company is out of state, then you need to look for their register agent in your state. Once you find the agent, you can have them served with the notice of complaint. Do a search on the Better Business Bureau website and on www.residentagentinfo.com to locate the agent of the business?

How do I prepare for the trial?

You can prepare your evidence by getting a copy of the laws, outlining your argument, and learning what the credit bureau or collection agency may present at the day of court. Thoroughly organize and study your evidence. You will need to prep your witnesses, put your recordings in order, review your journal of notes from the credit bureau or collection agencies, pull your phone records, and review any medical records for proof of emotional distress. Review the laws that were violated and take a highlighted copy with you to court for the judge to review. Outline the events that took place step-by-step. You can even practice presenting your argument to the judge in front of a mirror.

What goes on in the hearing?

You should arrive early and dress professionally, as there will be others in the court also trying their cases. The clerk will call the role from the docket to see who is there. If only the plaintiff is present (meaning you), the judge will issue a default judgment awarding you the case automatically. If the defendant (the credit bureau or collection agency or creditor) is the only person to show up, the case will be dismissed. The judge will ask the parties to try in settle their matter with a mediator waiting outside in the hallway. If a settlement is unsuccessful, your case will be heard in order. When your case is called, you and the defendant will present arguments to the judge, and after hearing both sides of the story, the judge will deliver a decision right away or later by mail.

What happens if I don't win the case? Do I risk losing anything?

If you don't win your case, you may have to pay the defendant's attorney fees if the small claims court in your area allows those fees to be collected from the defendant (the company you are suing), so check with the small claims court about this issue before filing your case. Furthermore, you will lose your filing fee, and any money you used to bring the case to court. In addition, the defendant can try to collect any fees, they accumulated trying to defend the case against you.

If I lose, will any fees be added to my negative account balance?

No. There will be no additional fees added to your balance, unless the original contract you signed with the creditor allows for legal fees to be collected. Read through your contract before taking your creditor to court to better understand what they can collect if you lose the case. Now if you are suing the creditor bureau or the collection agency, then their general fees to defend against the suit will apply in this situation.

Key points to remember

- Review the FCRA and FDCPA
- Consult an attorney for guidance
- Try to settle the case out of court first
- Bring your action before the statute expires
- Do legal research in the law library or online
- Keep your evidence in order
- Visit the court and sit in on a case for experience

Q&A

What is the Right of Offset Law?

With this law or clause in your banking agreement, it gives the lender the authority to dig into your checking or savings account and pull out the late payments. They can do this because they hold your outstanding loan and checking accounts all under one roof.

What are Usury Laws?

Each state has usury laws that place caps on interest rates for credit card companies, banks, and payday lenders. For example, if your loan is turned over to a collection agency, the usury law kicks in and you would only have to pay the interest allowed by the state, which is lower than what the bank was previous charging you.

What is a confession of judgment?

Confession of judgment will allow the lender to get a judgment against you without suing you. Make sure not to sign any loan agreements with this clause inside.

What is a dragnet clause?

Under a dragnet clause, your current financial institution may confiscate your car to pay for other delinquent accounts you have with the same lender. Even though your car loan may not be the loan in question, the bank can still take it to satisfy other outstanding debts. It is a cross collateralization system, and it is mostly used by credit unions when you have obtained a car loan.

If I don't dispute the negative items, when will they come off?

According to the FCRA, most negatives trade lines must automatically come off your credit report after seven years from the date the account went delinquent except for bankruptcies, unpaid tax liens, and renewed judgments. **See the Federal law statutes in the appendix**

Why can a mortgage lender see all of my deleted debts?

Say you had bad credit, and you cleaned it up, then later down the road you applied for a job, insurance, or a transaction with an amount over 75,000 a year. Those old deleted accounts could be exposed to your future grantor.

Why is my credit history missing from my credit report?

Some lenders may not report your good credit history because they are afraid their competition may see your excellent paying history and start offering you credit through pre-approve applications. Make sure when you check your credit reports that your lender is always reporting the correct information about your account.

Can you tell me why my credit card was canceled?

A credit card company may cancel your card if there is no activity on your account for up to 18 months. The reason for this is you are not making the credit card company any money. You can avoid this by having a certain amount of money taking out of your credit card account every month like your cell phone or utility bill.

Can I pay the creditor, and dispute later?

Yes, to avoid a major hit on your credit report, pay the debt that the creditor is claiming you owe after having them validate it, then dispute it with them later. If you don't pay the debt, it will go onto your credit report and damage it for seven years. You will then have to spend years trying to fix it, and as you can see it's not worth the trouble.

Why has the credit bureau extended my dispute?

If you supply the credit bureau with additional information during your 30-day waiting period, the credit bureau could extend their investigation by another 15 days according to the FCRA.

Is it hard to verify old debts?

The older the trade line is the more difficult it will be for the credit bureau to verify it as this usually happens due to a lack of records from the creditor.

How did the collection agencies track me down?

Whenever you fill out any type of financial application, this information goes straight to the credit bureau. This is how the collectors obtain your personal information like your social security number, date of birth, address, current employer, and past employer. The collection agencies and attorneys use this information to track you down if you default on your obligations.

Why is the same negative account on my credit report three times?

These incorrect trade lines can be placed on your credit report three times which is violation of the law. For example, the creditor will charge off the balance as a bad debt, and it will appear on your credit report as a charge off. Then the debt would be sold to a collection agency, and they will put the same account on your credit report as a collection. If they can't collect, they will have an attorney sue and a judgment will appear on your credit report. You see how this one account can hurt your report three times. Follow the normal dispute process to handle this matter and let the credit bureau and the collection agency know that they are violating the law.

A deleted item came back onto my credit report.

If you notice that an item that was previously deleted, and it is now back on your credit report, it is perfectly legal as long as the credit bureau notified you within five days before they place the incorrect item on your report. Here is what happen, the credit bureau sent out a validation letter to the creditor, and for some reason, the creditor did not validate the debt within 30 days, so the debt was deleted. Ten days later, the creditor verified the debt, and it was placed back onto your report.

What is Universal Default?

This is a clause buried in your credit card contract, which allows the creditor to raise your interest rates for any reason. Did you know that this clause was in your contract? Did you read the fine print? Believe it or not, here is what your credit card company can do according to the Universal Default Clause: if you are late on a credit card issued to you by another bank, your current credit card company can raise your interest rates to the max.

Is the date of last activity important?

Yes. When the creditor sells your debt to a collection agency, it can reset the federal statute of limitation on that particular debt. For example, if the creditor reports your account negative on March 3, 2010, to the credit bureau, according to the federal statute of limitation, this account should fall off your credit report on 2017, but if the creditor sells the bad debt to a collection agency on March 3, 2011, the statute restarts and now the negative items fall off on March 3, 2018. This is a violation of the FCRA, and you can use the violation as an argument when disputing item.

Why is a bankruptcy appearing on my credit report?

If you start the proceedings to file for bankruptcy, and you stop right in the middle of filing, your credit report will show the bankruptcy. The fact that there was a commencement could place the bankruptcy on your report for 10 years. Check your credit report and talk with your bankruptcy attorney about this procedure.

I noticed multiple listings on my credit report.

The Fair Credit Reporting Act requires that you have no more than one listing per account on your credit report. The creditor can report you late, but the collection agency can't turn around and report the same account as being behind. If this happens, it's against the law, and you must let the credit bureau and collection agency know that through a demanding letter. Furthermore, advise them if it's not deleted, you will be notifying the Attorney General's office.

Glossary

Attorney General

Chief attorney of a state and head of its legal department.

Authorized user

A person who is allowed to charge items on another person's credit card without being held responsible for paying back the debt.

Credit Bureau

Firm that monitors the creditworthiness and assigns a credit rating to a consumer.

Credit report

A report containing the details of your credit history.

Collections

When an account goes past-due after three months, it is transferred to an in-house or third-party company to attempt to collect the debt.

Charge off

When the bank can no longer collect on a debt, it writes off the account as a bad debt.

Child support

Payments paid to a divorced spouse or guardian for the care of a child who is still a minor.

Collection agency

A third-party company hired by a creditor to collect unpaid debts from a consumer. The collection agency gets a percentage of what it collects.

Check system

A company that maintains records of bad check writing and outstanding debt owed to the banks. Banks use this company when a consumer applies for a checking account.

Credit monitoring

A service that monitors the activity on your credit report. When there is activity, the company will notify the consumer by email or text.

Court of equity

Courthouse having jurisdiction in equity.

Civil complaint

Civil action, presenting a cause of action against another person.

Credit card

A card that extends credit to a person which allows him to buy items and he/she is billed on that charge.

Credit freeze

Freezes up the consumers credit report to prevent new accounts from being open.

Community state

A state that makes a husband and wife responsible for each others debts.

Cosigner

I joint signer of a promissory note make the signer responsible for the debt if the original owner defaults.

Delinquent accounts

If your payment is not received on the due date, then it's considered delinquent

Defendant

A person who is defending themself against a complaint brought on in court.

Divorce decree

The court's order of termination for a marriage.

Deficiency judgment

Money judgment issued for the amount not covered after the sale of an item like a car or a house.

Expansion score

Predicts credit worthiness for consumers without FICO scores using non-traditional methods like utility bills, rent payments and cell phone payments.

Fair Credit Reporting Act

A Federal law that regulates the credit bureaus.

Fair Debt Collection Practices Act

Federal law that regulates third-party collection agencies.

Federal Trade Commission

An organization that promotes consumer protection.

Fraud alert

A consumer places a security alert on his credit report when he as been a victim of identity theft. Whenever someone tries to open up an account with the consumer's social security number, the consumer is notified.

FICO score

A three-digit number drawn up from the consumer credit report. Lenders use this number to determine whether to grant a consumer credit.

File a motion

An oral or written request made to the court requesting the judge to direct a certain act to be done in favor of the applicant.

Foreclosure

When an owner of a home defaults on their loan, their rights to own that property are terminated. This will result in a force sale of the home in a public auction.

Hearing

A proceeding heard before a judge.

Injunctive relief

A court order prohibiting an act.

Inquiries

An indication on your credit report indicating each time you or a creditor pulled your credit report.

Joint account

An agreement detailing that both parties will be responsible for the account.

Judgment proof

A person who is financially insolvent and therefore without the funds or assets to pay his or her outstanding debts.

Legal summons

An official order to appear in court to answer a complaint.

Money damages

When the court awards money if a consumer wins a liability suit.

Public records

Records which a government entity is required to maintain.

Passbook loan

Funds secured by a savings account. The money cannot be taken out during the life of the loan.

Plaintiff

A person who brings on a lawsuit by filing a complaint against a second party.

Post dated check

A check written to be cashed on a certain date.

Repossession

Using the courts to take back property that is secured by a loan.

Re-aged account

When a customer is late on multiple payments, the lender can change the accounts from delinquent to current.

Register agent

The person responsible for receiving and sending legal papers on behalf of a business.

Suppress

To close or keep from appearing or being known.

Debt settlement

Settling a debt for less than the original amount.

Skip tracing

Locating the whereabouts of a particular person.

Secured debt

A debt secured by collateral. For example, the car secures a car loan.

Statute of limitation

A federal or state statute that restricts the amount of time legal proceedings could be brought against a person or a company.

Tax lien

A lien placed on a property to secure the payment for taxes. So once the property is sold, the tax liens must be paid first.

Three-in-one credit report

A credit report that contains information from all three credit reports at one time.

Technicality

Technical aspect of the law.

Unsecured debt

Where there is no collateral against the debt in case the consumer defaults.

Verification

Confirming something to be true.

Validation

To make something legally valid.

Writ

A written directive by the court ordering the party to perform a certain act.

Appendix

Sample dispute track form

Dispute Tracking Sheet

Letter sent	Date sent	Item disputed	Their response	Notes

Letter sent	Date sent	Item disputed	Their response	Notes

Letter sent	Date sent	Item disputed	Their response	Notes

Additional dispute letters

Follow up dispute letter one

Send this letter when the credit bureau has not responded to your first dispute letter after 30 days.

My Full name:
My Address:
My Date of Birth:
My Social Security number:
Report Number:
Date:

Dear Credit Bureau
Thirty days ago, I sent your company a letter disputing the items listed below (see certified return receipts and prior letter attached). As of today, your company has failed to respond. According to the FCRA, you have 30 days to investigate, and if you cannot verify the inaccurate information listed, it must be deleted from my credit report.
Account one:
Account two:
Account three:
Please delete this misleading information and supply me with a corrected credit report within 30 days.

Sincerely,
Print your name here.
Sign your name here.

Follow up dispute letter two

Send this letter when the credit bureau did not respond to your first letter or your second letter.

My Full name:
My Address:
My Date of Birth:
My Social Security number:
Report Number:
Date:

Dear Credit Bureau

You have failed to respond to the first and second letter, which is a clear violation of the FCRA. As of today, it has been 60 days since I sent out my first letter (see certified return receipt and prior letter attached). The FCRA requires that you investigate all disputes initiated by the consumer. I demand that you delete the inaccurate trade lines listed below.

Account one:
Account two:
Account three:

Please delete this misleading information, and supply me with a corrected credit report within 30 days. If, for some reason, I don't receive a return response within 10 days, I will file a complaint with the Office of the Attorney General.

Sincerely,
Print your name here.
Sign your name here.

Frivolous letter response

Send this letter when the credit bureau thinks that your disputes are frivolous.

My Full name:
My Address:
My Date of Birth:
My Social Security number:
Report Number:
Date:

Dear Credit Bureau,
I just received your letter deeming disputes being frivolous. Please send me a response explaining how you came to this decision. In addition, I would like to remind you that the FCRA requires you to investigate disputes initiated by consumers, and I expect your company to comply with the law by reinvestigating the items listed below:
Account one:
Account two:
Account three:
Please delete this misleading information and supply me with a corrected credit report within 30 days. If, for some reason, I don't receive a return response within 10 days, I will file a complaint with the Office of the Attorney General.

Sincerely,
Print your name here.
Sign your name here.

Credit Repair Company

Send this letter if the credit bureau states that you are working with a credit repair company.

My Full name:
My Address:
My Date of Birth:
My Social Security number:
Report Number:
Date:

Dear Credit Bureau,
After reviewing your letter, I would like to say that I am not using a credit repair firm and never have. I feel that the items listed below are inaccurate, and I would like for your company to investigate.
Account one:
Account two:
Account three:
Please delete this misleading information, and supply me with a corrected credit report within 30 days. If, for some reason, I don't receive a return response within 10 days, I will file a complaint with the Office of the Attorney General.

Sincerely,
Print your name here.
Sign your name here.

Complain to the FTC

Send this letter after you have advised the credit bureau that you will file a complaint with the FTC.

My Full name:
My Address:
Date:

Dear FTC
I have written to (name of credit bureau here) on several occasions disputing the fact that the items listed below are incorrect. The credit bureau has either refused to respond, sent a frivolous letter, sent a "working with a credit repair company letter," or continues to state that they have verified the debt. Let this be a formal complaint against the (the name of the credit bureau goes here). The following accounts are the items the credit bureau has refused to investigate.
Account one:
Account two:
Account three:

Sincerely,
Print your name here.
Sign your name here.

Get a copy of your credit report

Use this letter to request a copy of your credit report.

My Full name:
My Address:
My Date of Birth:
My Social Security number:
Report Number:
Date:

Dear Credit Bureau

I would like to receive my credit report. Included with this letter is a copy of my driver's license, social security card, and a current utility bill. Please mail the report to the address listed above.

Sincerely,
Print your name here.
Sign your name here.

Good Will Letter

Send this letter to the creditor when you are trying to get a late payment removed from your credit report.

Your name:
Your address:
Address of the creditor or the collection agency:
Date:
Reference account number:

Dear creditor,
I apologize for the recent lateness in my payments. I was recently laid off from my job and the financial duress has caused me to fall behind on my payments. As your records indicate, I have been an excellent customer with a good payment history until the economy took a dive. I enjoy being a loyal credit card customer of your company, and would greatly appreciate if you gave me another chance by deleting the 90-day late mark on my credit report. Thank you for taking the time to reading my letter.

Sincerely,
Your signature here.

Sample settlement letters

First settlement letter

Send this letter when you are first trying to settle by mail.

Your name:
Your address:
Address of creditor or collection agency:
Date:
Reference account number:

Dear creditor or collection agency,
Currently, and in the past, I have undergone tremendous financial difficulty. The overwhelming nature of my financial situation has even forced me to consider filing for bankruptcy. I have talked with all of my creditors, and they have agreed to settle all of my unsecured debts for 30 cents on the dollar, as this is all the money I have with no assets. For full payment of my debts, I am asking your company to remove the negative items listed on my credit report. If you agree to my terms, I will gladly send you a payment after receipt of your acknowledgement.
Thank you so much for your time and your hopeful cooperation,

Your signature here.

Second settlement letter

This is another version of a settlement letter.

Your name:
Your address:
Address of creditor or collection agency:
Date:
Reference account number:

Dear creditor or collection agency,
Please let me explain why I have not paid the outstanding debt. For the last year, I have been living on unemployment trying to secure a new job, so that I could catch up on my bills. Finally, I secured employment, and I'm now ready to settle my debts. I have offered a settlement to other creditors who have agreed to the terms, and I would like to offer you the same settlement of 20 cents on the dollar with a complete deletion of negative information on my credit report. If you agree to these terms, please fax or mail back a signed agreement and I will send out the payment right away.

Sincerely,
Your signature here.

Third settlement letter

Send this letter when you are trying to settle by mail.

Your name:
Your address:
Address of the creditor or collection agency:
Date:
Reference account number:

Dear creditor or collection agency,
For the last year, I have been in financial crises with a zero savings. Recently, I've obtained employment, and now I am ready to settle these outstanding debts. Currently, I am in negotiations with other creditors who have agreed to take 20 cents on the dollar because that is all the money I have before filing for bankruptcy. They also have agreed to remove any negative information reporting on my credit report. I would like to offer you the same deal and ask that you please remove any negative marks from my credit report. If you agree to the proposed terms, I will mail the payment when I receive a signed agreement.

Sincerely,
Your signature here.

Counter Offer

Send this letter to counter the creditor's offer.

Your name:
Your address:
Address of the creditor or the collection agency:
Date:
Reference account number:

Dear creditor or collection agency,
I would like to thank you for considering my early settlement letter, but at this time, I cannot come up with the money that you are asking for. I can settle for 23 cents on the dollar, as this is the only money I have. I'm in negotiations with other creditors with similar deals. If you can remove the negative information from my report, I will pay the debt at 23 cents on the dollar (put a whole dollar amount here) on the dollar by overnight mail.

Sincerely,
Your signature here.

Fifth settlement letter

Send this letter when you are trying to settle.

Your name:
Your address:
Address of the creditor or the collection agency:
Date:
Reference account number:

Dear creditor or collection agency,
In the last six months, I have been facing hard times with a lost of my job, my mother passing away and my brother going to jail. I sincerely apologize for falling behind on my debts, but I assure you my neglectfulness was circumstantial. Now that I have a job, I'm ready to settle my outstanding debt, and I would like to offer you 20 cents on the dollar (put a dollar amount here) for a deletion of all negative information from my credit report and no further collection activities. Currently, I'm in negotiations with other creditors on a similar deal, and I would like to close my account with you fast. If I receive a signed agreement from you, I will gladly send payment out overnight.

Sincerely,
Your signature here.

Letters to fight Collection agencies

Validation Letter one

Send this letter in order to have the creditor or the collection agency validate (or prove) the debt you owe.

Date:
Certified Mail
Return Receipt Requested:
Collection Agency address:
Your name:
Your address:
Reference account:

Dear Sir or Madam:
I just received a letter from your company stating that I owe an outstanding balance (see your letter attached). This letter is not a refusal to pay, however, I would like to let your company know that I am disputing your claim. Under the FDCPA, I am allowed to request verification from third party collection agencies. As you know, not complying with FDCPA will put your company in a bad position with the FTC, so I am asking that your company supply me with a copy of the following:

1. Proof that you either own or were assigned the debt from the creditor
2. Proof that you have the right to collect this debt in my state
3. Proof that your company carries a bond
4. Proof on how your company assessed the outstanding debt
5. Payment history from the original creditor
6. Name and address from the original creditor
7. Copy of the original contract bearing my signature

Thank you for your time and cooperation,
Your signature here.

Follow up validation letter

Send this letter if the creditor or the collection agency do not respond to your first letter.

Date:
Certified Mail
Return Receipt Requested:
Collection Agency address:
Your name:
Your address:
Reference account:

Dear Sir or Madam:
I sent your company a validation letter on (list date for previous letter sent). Since then, 30 days have passed, and I have not heard from your company. I'm aware of my rights, and unfortunately, you are still reporting negative items on my credit report. This is a clear violation of the FDCPA, which carries a penalty of $1,000 for every violation. If this incorrect item is not deleted from my account in 10 days, I have no other choice but to file a complaint with the FTC, attorney general's office and seek legal advice. Please see attached letter and certified return receipt mailing.

Sincerely,
Your signature here.

Cease and Desist Letter

Send this letter to force the collection agency stop calling or writing you.

Date:
Certified Mail
Return Receipt Requested:
Collection Agency address:
Your name:
Your address:
Reference account:

Dear Sir or Madam:
For the past 30 days, I have been receiving phone calls from various collectors working in your company. Each time I try to get information from the collector, the agency refuses to give me contact information. I have kept a written record of every phone call, which estimates to 30 and counting. Effective today, I would like for your company to stop calling and writing me. In accordance to FDCPA guidelines against harassment, I will be forced to take legal action if harassed any longer.

Sincerely,
Your signature here.

Sample legal forms

Motion to vacate a judgment

_____ (Name of Court)
State of _____ County of _____

Small Claims Part
_____ Plaintiff,

Against

_____ Defendant,

Comes now_____ Defendant, in the above-styled cause, and respectfully requests that this Honorable Court set aside the Default and Default Judgment entered in this cause   on   the   _____day   the   _____day of_____, _____,

I did not appear because

_____

_____

WHEREFORE, Defendant moves this Honorable Court for an Order setting aside the Default and Default Judgment previously entered.

Defendant's Signature

_____
Defendant's Address and telephone number

_____

Satisfaction of Judgment

Send this letter to the court when your judgment is paid.

IN THE JUSTICE COURT OF _____
TOWNSHIP
STATE OF_____
NAME: _____ ,
CASE NO: _____
_____

Plaintiff
vs
Satisfaction of Judgment
_____
Defendant,

The Plaintiff hereby acknowledges that the Judgment entered on the____ day of _____, _____, along with all cost in the above-entitled action, has been satisfied. Accordingly, I herby authorize and direct the Court to note this Satisfaction of Judgment.

Per the Statute, "I declare under penalty of perjury that the foregoing is true and correct."

Executed on _____,_____ (Date)
_____(Signature)

Sample Small Claims Complaint

This is what a lawsuit complaint looks like.

Justice Court, _____Township
Name: _____
Case No. _____
Address: _____
AFFIDAVIT OF COMPLAINT
SMALL CLAIMS

_____
Plaintiff
VS
NAME: _____
ADDRESS: _____
_____
Defendant
STATE OF_____
COUNTY OF_____
_____, being duly
sworn, states that the Defendant owes the Plaintiff the sum of
$_____ for

_____
That demand for payment has been made; the defendant refuses to
pay, that the Defendant either resides, works or does business in the
Township of_____, County, State.

SUBSCRIBED AND SWORN to before me this _____ day
of_____, _____
Plaintiff: _____
Phone Number: _____
NOTARY PUBLIC: _____
Date: _____
OR: ONE OF THE FOLLOWING: Per Statute
if executed in this state: "I declare under penalty of perjury that the
foregoing is true and correct."
Executed on_____, _____ (Date)
_____(Signature)
If executed outside of this state (_____): "I declare under
penalty of perjury under the law of the state of Nevada that the
foregoing is true and correct."

Laws and Debt

Federal Statute of limitation for Negative items on your credit report

Statute starts 180 days from the day the account became delinquent

CREDIT ITEM	TIME LIMIT/YEARS	STATE RETENTION RULE
Chapter 13 bankruptcy	7	N/A
Chapter 7	10	N/A
Civil Suit	7	N/A
Judgment	7	NY 5 years from the date it was filed
Paid Tax lien	7	CA 10 years from the date filed
Unpaid Tax lien	Not specified by federal law	CA 10 years from the date filed
Collection account	7	NY 5 years
Charge - offs and Repossessions	7	NY 5 years
Late payments	7	N/A
Employment Inquiries	2	N/A
Inquiries	1	N/A

Statute of limitation on debts

Statute starts the day the account was open

Wage garnishment exemption

STATE	OPEN ACCOUNT CREDIT CARDS (years)	WRITTEN ACCOUNTS LOANS (years)	WAGE GARNISHMENT EXEMPTION
Alabama	3	6	75% of wages are exempt from garnishment
Alaska	4	6	75% of employee's weekly net income
Arizona	3	6	75% of wages are exempt
Arkansas	3	5	$500 head of family, $200 if single
California	4	4	75% of wages are exempt
Colorado	3	6	75% of wages are exempt
Connecticut	6	6	25% of disposable earnings
Delaware	4	3	85% of disposable earnings
District of Columbia	3	3	75% of wages are exempt
Florida	4	5	Head of house hold 100% of wages are exempt if not 75% is exempt
Georgia	4	6	75% of wages are exempt
Hawaii	6	6	75% of wages are exempt

Idaho	4	4	75% of wages are exempt
Illinois	5	10	15% of gross wages
Indiana	6	6	75% of wages are exempt
Iowa	5	10	75% of wages are exempt
Kansas	3	5	75% of wages are exempt
Kentucky	5	15	75% of wages are exempt
Louisiana	3	10	75% of wages are exempt
Maine	6	6	25% of disposable income
Maryland	3	3	75% of wages are exempt
Massachusetts	6	6	$125 per week
Michigan	6	6	75% of wages are exempt
Minnesota	6	6	75% of wages are exempt
Mississippi	3	3	75% of wages are exempt
Missouri	5	10	90% net earnings if head of household
Montana	5	8	75% of wages are exempt
Nebraska	4	5	75% of wages are exempt
Nevada	4	8	25% of disposable earnings
New Hampshire	3	3	50 times the federal minimum hourly wage
New Jersey	8	8	May not exceed 10% of gross salary
New Mexico	4	6	75% of wages are exempt

State			
New York	6	6	Ten percent (10%) of gross income
North Carolina	3	3	Not granted to general creditors
North Dakota	6	6	75% of wages are exempt
Ohio	4	15	75% of wages are exempt
Oklahoma	3	5	75% of wages are exempt
Oregon	6	6	75% of wages are exempt
Pennsylvania	4	4	100% of wages exempt
Rhode Island	10	10	75% of wages exempt
South Carolina	3	3	100 percent of wages exempt
South Dakota	6	6	20% of the individuals earnings for a 60 day period
Tennessee	6	6	75% of wages exempt
Texas	4	4	$142.50 of disposable weekly earnings
Utah	4	6	75% of wages exempt
Vermont	6	6	75% of wages exempt
Virginia	3	5	75% of wages exempt
Washington	3	6	75% of wages exempt
West Virginia	5	10	20% of disposable income
Wisconsin	6	6	80 percent of net earnings
Wyoming	8	10	75% of wages exempt

Statute of limitation for judgments

STATE	SOL (years)	%INTEREST RATE ALLOWED ON JUDGMENTS
AL	20	12
AR	10	10.5
AK	5	10
AZ	10	5 ABOVE FEDERAL RATE
CA	10	10
CO	20	8
CT	20	10
DE	NONE	LEGAL + FED DISCOUNT + 5%
DC	3	70% OF INTEREST RATE OR 6% IF NOT SPECIFIED
FL	20	10
GA	7	12
HI	10	10
IA	6	10.875
ID	20	9
IL	20	8
IN	20	10

KS	5	4%
KY	15	12
LA	10	9.75
ME	20	15% IF UNDER 30 MONTHS
MD	12	10
MA	20	12
MI	10	6.953
MN	10	5%, CHANGES YEARLY
MS	7	AMOUNT IN THE CONTRACT
MO	10	9
MT	10	10
NC	5	1% ABOVE BOND EQUIVALENT YIELD
ND	6	2% ABOVE THE PRIME RATE
NE	20	10
NH	20	NO PROVISIONS
NJ	14	8.75% WITHOUT A WRITTEN CONTRACT
NM	20	9
NV	10	8
NY	10	12

OH	21	10
OK	5	4% OVER THE T-BILL RATE
OR	10	9% RENEWABLE AT 10 YEARS
PA	4	6
RI	20	12
SC	10	14
SD	20	10
TN	10	10
TX	10	6
UT	8	JUDGMENT CONTRACT RATE
VA	8	12
VT	20	9
WA	10	12
WI	10	10

HUD's Time Guidelines on Foreclosures

STATE	DAYS BEFORE FORECLOSURE BEGINS (days)
Alabama	85
Alaska	140
Arizona	125
Arkansas	130
California	135
Colorado	130
Connecticut	220
Delaware	250
Florida	170
Georgia	80
Guam	250
Hawaii	140
Nebraska	155
Nevada	111
New Hampshire	110
New Jersey	300
New Mexico	250
New York	280
North Carolina	120
North Dakota	190
Ohio	265
Oklahoma	250
Oregon	180
Pennsylvania	300
Illinois	275
Indiana	265
Iowa	315

Kansas	180
Kentucky	265
Louisiana	220
Maine	355
Maryland	85
Massachusetts	135
Michigan	75
Minnesota	110
Mississippi	130
Missouri	85
Montana	205
Rhode Island	85
South Carolina	215
South Dakota	205
Tennessee	90
Texas	90
Utah	165
Vermont	360
Virgin Isles	325
Virginia	60
Washington	160
West Virginia	145
Wisconsin	310
Wyoming	100

States where collectors can't and can collect the difference

CAN'T COLLECT	CAN COLLECT
Arkansas	Alabama
Colorado	Delaware
Connecticut	Massachusetts
Georgia	Minnesota
Louisiana	Missouri
Main	New Hampshire
Michigan	New York
Nebraska	Ohio
New Jersey	Road Island
North Carolina	South Carolina
Oregon	South Dakota
Pennsylvania	West Virginia
Texas	Wisconsin

States and small claims courts

STATE	MONEY LIMIT	STATE	MONEY LIMIT
Alabama	3,000	Indiana	6,000
Alaska	10,000	Iowa	5,000
Arizona	2,500	Kansas	4,000
Arkansas	5,000	Kentucky	1,500
California	7,500	Louisiana	3,000
Colorado	7,500	Maine	4,500
Connecticut	5,000	Maryland	5,000
Delaware	15,000	Massachusetts	2,000
District of Columbia	5,000	Michigan	3,000
Florida	5,000	Minnesota	7,500
Georgia	15,000	Mississippi	3,500
Hawaii	3,500	Missouri	3,000
Idaho	5,000	Montana	3,000
Illinois	10,000	Nebraska	2,700

Nevada	5,000	New Hampshire	7,500
New Jersey	3,000	New Mexico	10,000
New York	5,000	North Carolina	5,000
North Dakota	5,000	Ohio	3,000
Oklahoma	6,000	Oregon	7,500
Pennsylvania	10,000	Rhode Island	2,500
South Carolina	7,500	South Dakota	12,000
Tennessee	15,000	Texas	10,000
Utah	10,000	Vermont	5,000
Virginia	5,000	Washington	5,000
West Virginia	5,000	Wisconsin	5,000
Wyoming	7,000	Wyoming	7,000

States and recording phone calls

One party states

ONE PARTY STATE	ONE PARTY STATE	ONE PARTY STATE	ONE PARTY STATE
Alaska	Arkansas	Colorado	Iowa
District of Columbia	Georgia	Florida	Kansas
Hawaii	Idaho	Indiana	Kentucky
Louisiana	Maine	Minnesota	Mississippi
Missouri	Nebraska	Nevada	New Jersey
New Mexico	New York	North Carolina	North Dakota
Ohio	Oregon	Oklahoma	Rhode Island
South Carolina	Tennessee	Texas	Utah
Vermont	Virginia	Washington	West Virginia
Wisconsin	Wyoming	Wisconsin	Wyoming

Two party states

TWO PARTY STATES	TWO PARTY STATES	TWO PARTY STATES	TWO PARTY STATES
California	Connecticut	Delaware	Florida
Illinois	Maryland	Massachusetts	Michigan
Montana	New Hampshire	Pennsylvania	California

Laws and Collection Agencies

STATE	STATUTE	STATE	STATUTE
Alabama	40-12-80	Alaska	24.0.011
Arizona	32-1001	Arkansas	617-21-104
California	1788	Colorado	5-10101
Connecticut	36-243	Delaware	30, 2301(13)
District of Columbia	22-3423	Florida	559.55
Georgia	7-3-1	Hawaii	443-B-1
Idaho	26-2222	Illinois	2001
Indiana	25-11-1-1	Iowa	537-7101
Kansas	16a-5-107	Kentucky	None
Louisiana	9.3510	Maine	Title 32-11,001
Maryland	56-323	Massachusetts	Chapter 93, 24
Michigan	19.655	Minnesota	None
Minnesota	None	Missouri	None
Montana	None	Nebraska	45-601
Nevada	649-005	New Hampshire	358-C,1
New Jersey	45,18-1	New Mexico	61-18A-1
New York	600	North Carolina	66-49.24
North Dakota	13-05-01	Ohio	None
Oklahoma	None	Oregon	646.639
Pennsylvania	7311,201-1	Rhode Island	None
South Carolina	37-5-108	South Dakota	None
Tennessee	62-20-101	Texas	5069-11.01
Utah	12-1-1	Vermont	Title 9-2451a
Virginia	18.2	Washington	19.16.100
West Virginia	47-16-1	Wisconsin	218.04
Wisconsin	218.04	Wyoming	33-11-101

Dispute Letters in Microsoft Word Format at
Hiddencreditrepairsecrets.com

Resources

Credit bureaus

Experian NCAC, PO BOX 9701, ALLEN, TX 75013
888-397-3742
www.experian.com

Equifax, PO BOX 105518, ATLANTA, GA 30348
800-685-1111
www.equifax.com

Trans Union, PO BOX 2000,CHESTER, PA 19022
800-916-8800
www.transunion.com

Innovis Data Solutions, 950 Threadneedle St., Suite 200
Houston TX 77079-2903

Annual Credit Report, P.O. Box 105281, Atlanta,
GA 30348-5281.
877-322-8228
www.annualcreditreport.com

Sending dispute online

www.stamps.com

www.endicia.com

If retail stores, creditors, credit bureaus or debt collectors refuse to assist you with your problem, write to:

Federal Trade Commission
www.ftc.gov
Consumer Response Center 1-877-FTC-Help
Consumer Protection Hotline 1-800-621-0508
Division of Credit Practices:
Federal Trade Commission
Washington, DC 20580

Problems with National banks

Office of the Comptroller of the Currency Deputy Comptroller of Customer and Commuting programs
Department of the Treasury, 6th Floor
L'Enfant Plaza
Washington, DC 20219

Problems with State member banks

Federal Reserve Board
Division of Consumer and Community Affairs
20th and C Street, N.W.
Washington, DC 20551

Problems with a credit union:

National Credit Union Administration
Office of Consumer Affairs
1776 G St., N.W.
Washington, DC 20456

The State Regulatory Agency

www.allthingspolitical.org/index.htm

Federal Deposit Insurance Corporation

www.fdic.gov/bank/analytical/firstfifty/

Comptroller of the Currency Federal Reserve System

www.occ.treas.gov/sites.htm

Rebuild your score with secured cards

www.bankrate.com

www.cardratings.com

www.creditcards.com

www.creditcardscenter.com

www.e-wisdom.com

www.lowermybills.com

Banks known to issue secured cards with low limits

Capitol One

First Premier

Orchard Bank

New Millennium Bank

Prbc.com

www.Prbc.com

Challenged credit personal loans

www.completeloansource.com

Consumers with challenged credit

www.carloans.com

www.isourcerents.com

Student loan information

For more information on Student loans contact the Federal Student Aid Information Center at 1-800-433-3243 or visit them at www.nslds.ed.gov. You can also contact the Direct Loan Servicing Center at 1-800-848-0979.

Help with your bills

American Credit Counselors
www.billfree.org

Community Credit Counselors
www.debt911.org

Consumer Credit Counseling
www.consumercounseling.org

Institute of Consumer Financial Education
www.ICFE.info

National Foundation for Credit Counseling
www.nfcc.org

Debtors Anonymous
www.debtorsanonymous.org

Bankruptcy exemption laws

www.nacba.org,

http://www.bankruptcyaction.com/nvexemptions.htm

Approved credit consumer counselors

www.moneymanagement.org

www.greenpathbk.com

Where can I find the means income standards?

www.usdoj.gov

www.justice.gov/ust/eo/bapcpa/meanstesting.htm

Lawyers and legal research

Lawyers: go to prepaidlegal.com and sign up for a membership.

Legal research: www.jurisearch.com www.versuslaw.com westlaw.com or lexisnexis.com

Resident agent: http://residentagentinfo.com/to

Sample motion

www.examplemotion.com

Car repossession laws

www.nfa.org

Foreclosure

Obama Plan-Harp-Home Affordable Modification Program
www.hmpadmin.com

Mortgage Debt Forgiveness Program
http://taxes.about.com/od/income/qt/canceled_debt.htm

Consumer laws

Fair Credit Reporting Act
www.ftc.gov

Fair Debt Collection Practices Act
www.ftc.gov

Truth in Lending Act
www.occ.gov/publications/publications

Equal Opportunity Act
www.dol.gov/

Recommended reading:

Think progress - by Skip J. Williams

!STOP!
JOIN THE COMMUNITY

AT

HIDDENCREDITREPAIRSECRETS.COM

FOR MORE POWERFUL CREDIT REPAIR SECRETS

Want more copies

If you would like to order additional copies or would like to get a copy for your family or friends, you can go to Amazon.com and order your copy there.

Options

Paperback $29.99

Ebook $19.99

Dispute letters in Microsoft format $19.99

!WIN A FREE CREDIT ANALYSIS!

Valued at $200

Send an email to Creditrepairquestions1@gmail.com
and tell me what you thought about the book.

Reviews

If you found this book to be beneficial, please consider posting a review of it on Amazon to let other potential readers know why you liked it.

INDEX

About the Author

After suffering from a poor credit report for years, Mark Clayborne went on a mission to study everything he could on restoring his credit. Concluding the extensive research, he repaired his credit report and learned various hidden secrets on how to improve a bad credit file. Now, he wants to share these strategies with the world and as a result **HIDDEN CREDIT REPAIR SECRETS** was created. Mark Clayborne is a Board Certified Credit Consultant and a graduate of the Virginia Commonwealth University. He holds a Bachelor's Degree in Criminal Justice and a paralegal diploma. Mark currently lives in sunny Florida with a beautiful wife and lovely daughter.